ONTENTS

Preface

York Notes are designed to give you a broader perspective on works of literature studied at GCSE and equivalent levels. We have carried out extensive research into the needs of the modern literature student prior to publishing this new edition. Our research showed that no existing series fully met students' requirements. Rather than present a single authoritative approach, we have provided alternative viewpoints, empowering students to reach their own interpretations of the text. York Notes provide a close examination of the work and include biographical and historical background, summaries, glossaries, analyses of characters, themes, structure and language, cultural connections and literary terms.

If you look at the Contents page you will see the structure for the series. However, there's no need to read from the beginning to the end as you would with a novel, play, poem or short story. Use the Notes in the way that suits you. Our aim is to help you with your understanding of the work, not to dictate how you should learn.

York Notes are written by English teachers and examiners, with an expert knowledge of the subject. They show you how to succeed in coursework and examination assignments, guiding you through the text and offering practical advice. Questions and comments will extend, test and reinforce your knowledge. Attractive colour design and illustrations improve clarity and understanding, making these Notes easy to use and handy for quick reference.

York Notes are ideal for:
- Essay writing
- Exam preparation
- Class discussion

The author of these Notes is David Pinnington. David read English at the universities of York and Exeter, where he took an MA in Modern Fiction. He teaches in Devon and is a Senior GCSE Examiner for English and English Literature.

The text used in these Notes is the Arden Shakespeare Series, edited by Frank Kermode, Nelson 1954, reprinted by Thomas Nelson & Sons Ltd, 1997.

Health Warning: **This study guide will enhance your understanding, but should not replace the reading of the original text and/or study in class.**

PART ONE

INTRODUCTION

HOW TO STUDY A PLAY

You have bought this book because you wanted to study a play on your own. This may supplement classwork.

- Drama is a special 'kind' of writing (the technical term is 'genre') because it needs a performance in the theatre to arrive at a full interpretation of its meaning. When reading a play you have to imagine how it should be performed; the words alone will not be sufficient. Think of gestures and movements.

- Drama is always about conflict of some sort (it may be below the surface). Identify the conflicts in the play and you will be close to identifying the large ideas or themes which bind all the parts together.

- Make careful notes on themes, characters, plot and any sub-plots of the play.

- Playwrights find non-realistic ways of allowing an audience to see into the minds and motives of their characters. The 'soliloquy', in which a character speaks directly to the audience, is one such device. Does the play you are studying have any such passages?

- Which characters do you like or dislike in the play? Why? Do your sympathies change as you see more of these characters?

- Think of the playwright writing the play. Why were these particular arrangements of events, these particular sets of characters and these particular speeches chosen?

Studying on your own requires self-discipline and a carefully thought-out work plan in order to be effective. Good luck.

Family life   William Shakespeare was born at Stratford-upon-Avon in 1564. There is a record of his christening, 26 April, so we can assume he was born shortly before that date. His father, John Shakespeare, was a glove-maker and trader who later became high bailiff of Stratford; his mother, Mary Arden, was the daughter of a landowner. It is probable that William would have attended the local grammar school where the curriculum included Latin rhetoric, logic and literature.

In 1582 Shakespeare married Anne Hathaway, a woman eight years older than himself, and their first child, Susanna, was christened in May 1583. Two other children were born to Anne and William in 1585, the twins Hamnet and Judith. Both Shakespeare's daughters lived to marry and produce children, but Hamnet only lived till he was eleven – his burial took place in Stratford on 11 August 1596.

Writing   Sometime after 1585 Shakespeare left Stratford and went to London where he became an actor and a dramatist. He worked first with a group of actors called Lord Pembroke's Men and later with a company called the Lord Chamberlain's Men (later the King's Men). His earliest plays, *Henry VI Parts 1–3, Richard III, Titus Andronicus* and the comedies *The Comedy of Errors, The Taming of the Shrew* and *The Two Gentlemen of Verona* were performed around 1590–4. Shakespeare was very successful in the theatre from the start and his genius inspired the resentment of one man, Robert Greene, a mediocre university-educated dramatist who described him to his friends as 'an upstart Crow, beautified with our feathers'.

In the 1590s Shakespeare wrote six more comedies, culminating in *Twelfth Night* in 1601. During this time he also wrote history plays, tragedies and the narrative poems, *Venus and Adonis* and *The Rape of Lucrece,* in addition to the Sonnets which were published in 1609.

In the early years of the new century he turned his attentions almost exclusively to **tragedy** and wrote some of the most powerful works in this **genre** (see Literary Terms) that have ever existed: *Hamlet* (1604–5), *Othello* (1604–5), *Macbeth* (1605–6), *King Lear* (1606–7) and *Antony and Cleopatra* (1606–7).

Although Shakespeare lived and worked for most of his life in London, he obviously did not forget Stratford. In 1596 he acquired the right to a coat of arms there, something his father had tried and failed to do, and in 1597 he bought a large house in the town called New Place. Later, in 1602, he acquired other property, and in about 1610 he returned to live in Stratford permanently.

The Tempest has been regarded as Shakespeare's farewell to the theatre.

Play-writing occupied Shakespeare until the final years of his life and between 1608–12 he produced the so-called 'last plays', *Pericles*, *Cymbeline*, *The Winter's Tale* and *The Tempest*. These plays suggest a mellowing in outlook and a concern for the relationships of parents and children, as if they were written by a man who was taking stock of his life and thinking of the future generation who would replace him.

Shakespeare wrote a will in January 1616, leaving bequests to Stratford acquaintances and to his actor-friends, Burbage, Heminges and Condell. The latter pair edited the first complete edition of Shakespeare's works, the First Folio of 1623. He died on 23 April 1616.

CONTEXT & SETTING

First performances

The Tempest was probably written as part of several entertainments to celebrate the betrothal of King James I's daughter Elizabeth to Frederick, Elector of the German Palatine States. The couple were married on

14 February 1613 and the play had been performed on two occasions at court in the preceding two years; it is likely that the date of composition is 1610–11.

Masques

The extreme artificiality of the **masque** (see Literary Terms) makes the surrounding action more credible. The fact that we know *The Tempest* was originally performed at court does not mean that it was written specifically for a royal audience, but it might explain the existence of masque elements in the play. The masque was a popular form of entertainment in the courts of Queen Elizabeth and King James. In *The Tempest* there are two masques: the miming masque in Act III and the wedding masque in Act IV. They show Shakespeare's ability to take the conventions of a well-known **genre** (see Literary Terms) and to integrate them within the main story of the play. There are **allegorical** (see Literary Terms) figures, stylised dialogue, music and dance, an opportunity for elaborate stage effects and scenery, classical deities and a theme celebrating marriage and fertility.

Sources

Shakespeare's practice as a writer was to derive his ideas for **plots** (see Literary Terms) from other sources. *The Tempest* reflects a number of elements which had existed in fairy tale, myth and folk tale a long time before Shakespeare was born, and there are similarities between the story and some features of the Commedia dell'Arte plays which were popular in sixteenth century Europe. However, two contemporary pieces of writing, which Shakespeare would have known, are analogous to the subject matter of *The Tempest*. These are Montaigne's essay, *Of Cannibals*, and the pamphlet published in 1610, *A Discovery of the Bermudas' otherwise called the Ile of Divels*. Montaigne's essay, translated by John Florio and published in 1603, reflects on the relative values of European and primitive societies. It is critical of the way 'civilised' societies interfere with the

workings of 'our great and puissant mother Nature' and
Michel de Montaigne describes a society where nature
alone governs:

> It is a nation ... that hath no kind of traffike, no knowledge of
> Letters, no intelligence of numbers, no name of magistrate,
> nor of politike superiorities; no use of service, of riches or of
> povertie; no contracts, no successions, no partitions, no occupation
> but idle; no respect of kindred, but common, no apparell but
> naturall, no manuring of lands, no use of wine, corne, or mettle.
> The very words that import lying, falsehood, treason,
> dissimulations, covetousness, envie, detraction, and pardon,
> were never heard of amongst them. How dissonant would
> hee [Plato] finde his imaginarie common-wealth from this
> perfection?'

The pamphlet describes the voyage to Virginia of a fleet
of nine ships which set out from England in May 1609.
A great storm broke out and the flagship disappeared.
The fleet sailed on for America and sent word back to
England that the ship was lost. After a year, in 1610,
the passengers and crew of the flagship arrived in
Virginia on two boats. During the storm their ship had
broken up on the shores of Bermuda and they had
survived unharmed. Contrary to popular belief at the
time, Bermuda turned out to be a hospitable natural
environment and the shipwrecked colonists had been
able to survive there for a year, eventually building
the boats which took them on to Virginia. This account
of their survival excited great interest in London in
1610 and aspects of it can be found reflected in *The
Tempest*.

Genre

The Tempest combines features of both **tragedy** and
comedy (see Literary Terms). In the idealised love
between Ferdinand and Miranda we find the focus on
the relationships of noble characters which is typical of
Shakespearean comedy. Another feature of comedy is
the separate comic **sub-plot** (see Literary Terms)

involving characters of lower status: this is represented in the activities of the servants, Caliban, Trinculo and Stephano.

However, there is a darker aspect to *The Tempest* which gives the play a potentially tragic dimension. Prospero is the victim of an act of evil treachery and we see the nature of this treachery in the actions of Antonio and Sebastian and it is echoed in Caliban's plot to murder Prospero. But in spite of the fact that these circumstances could lead to disaster, a tragic ending is avoided and reconciliation takes place.

Tragicomedy   In this *The Tempest* conforms to John Fletcher's definition of **tragicomedy** (see Literary Terms) from the preface to *The Faithful Sheperdess* (*c.*1610): 'A tragicomedy is not so called in respect of mirth and killing, but in respect it wants deaths, which is enough to make it no tragedy, yet brings some near it, which is enough to make it no comedy'.

Magic   Perhaps Shakespeare was thinking of Dr John Dee when he created the character of Prospero. He was a well-known Elizabethan mathematician and geographer who dabbled in magic and was thereby dubbed a 'magus'. In Shakespeare's England many people believed in the power of magic because life was harsh, especially for the uneducated, and science had not established itself as an explanatory system which was distinct from religion or the supernatural. The reformed church took away much of the mystery and magic associated with the Christian rites of the medieval church and because of this people were inclined to attribute supernatural powers to people who they thought could help them in times of trouble. In this sense, Prospero would have been a recognisable type to the original audience, a 'white' witch whose powers are used to serve an ultimate good.

The sea and
the storm

The Elizabethans believed they lived in an ordered universe where everything had its proper place in a God-given hierarchy. They believed that man was most in harmony with himself, with society and with God when he let his reason master his passions and accepted his allotted position in the hierarchy. They connected natural disasters, like storms or earthquakes, with disruptions to the equilibrium of states or individuals. In *The Tempest* the storm is a central **metaphor** (see Literary Terms) for the various disruptions which threaten or have taken place before the play begins. The audience is shown the moral degeneracy of those like Antonio who do not accept their place in the hierarchy and allow their ambition to destroy their conscience. The storm also signifies the moral battle implicit in the mind of Prospero. In the end he chooses the 'virtue' of forgiveness rather than vengeance, thus demonstrating that he has mastered his destructive passions. The sea has been an instrument of change for several of the characters in *The Tempest*, emptying them out of their orderly little world onto the shores of a magical island where, like the colonists of the time, their values and beliefs are challenged. Finally, the calmed sea reflects the restoration of rightful authority and order. As Ferdinand remarks, 'Though the seas threaten, they are merciful' (V.1.178).

PART TWO

SUMMARIES

GENERAL SUMMARY

Act I   The play begins with a storm at sea. The ship carrying Alonso, King of Naples, from his daughter's wedding in Tunis, breaks up on the shore of an island and all the passengers leap into the sea.

Prospero, the former Duke of Milan, is watching the shipwreck with his daughter, Miranda. They have been living on the island for twelve years. He tells her how he lost his dukedom to his brother, Antonio, who was helped in the plot by King Alonso. They had tried to get rid of Prospero and Miranda by casting them adrift at sea in a leaky boat. But a kindly old courtier, Gonzalo, had taken pity on them and put food and clothing in the boat, as well as some of the studious Prospero's beloved books. When they finally arrived on the island they found two inhabitants: Caliban, a deformed savage, and Ariel, a spirit imprisoned in a pine tree by Caliban's mother, the witch Sycorax who had died on the island before they arrived. Prospero found it impossible to educate Caliban and turned him into a slave after he tried to rape Miranda. Through the magic powers he had acquired from studying his books, Prospero released Ariel, having made the spirit promise to obey him. Indeed it is Ariel who has created the storm and shipwreck for Prospero, bringing the former duke's enemies to the island.

Prospero instructs Ariel to make himself invisible and to lure Ferdinand, Alonso's son, in the direction of Prospero's cell. Ferdinand is separated from the other passengers and believes his father has drowned in the shipwreck. When Miranda sees Ferdinand she thinks he is a divine spirit; Ferdinand, on the other hand, believes Miranda is a goddess. Prospero assures Miranda that Ferdinand is human and the young couple begin to fall in love. To make their love strong, Prospero pretends to believe that Ferdinand is a spy and takes him prisoner.

Act II In another part of the island Gonzalo attempts to comfort Alonso, who thinks Ferdinand is dead. Antonio and Sebastian mock Gonzalo and when the king and his counsellor fall asleep from exhaustion, Antonio persuades Sebastian that if they kill Alonso then and there, Sebastian, who is Alonso's brother, will be King of Naples. They draw their swords, but Ariel wakes the sleepers. Antonio and Sebastian pretend that they have heard the roaring of wild animals and have drawn their weapons to protect Alonso and Gonzalo. They are believed and the party continues to search for Ferdinand.

Caliban is carrying wood for Prospero. He hates his master and is frightened of his magical powers. He comes across two other members of Alonso's party who have survived the shipwreck: Trinculo, a jester, and Stephano, a drunken butler. When Stephano gives him some alcohol Caliban thinks it is some kind of heavenly liquor and that Stephano must be a god. He offers to serve Stephano and make the fertile island his kingdom. Rejoicing in his new master the drunken Caliban leads the two men away.

Act III Prospero has made Ferdinand carry logs as a punishment, a task the young man makes light of by consoling himself with thoughts of Miranda. When she comes to talk with him, secretly observed by Prospero, they declare their love and agree to marry. Prospero is delighted that his plan has worked.

Meanwhile, Caliban is explaining to Stephano how Prospero came to rule the island by magic and if

Time		Action
About 2pm *'The time 'twixt six and now Must by us both be spent most preciously'* Prospero I.2.240-1	**Act I**	The shipwreck; Prospero and Miranda watch; Miranda learns about Prospero's past. Ariel is reminded by Prospero of Sycorax and instructed to perform more tasks. Prospero and Miranda visit Caliban. Ariel lures Ferdinand to Prospero's cell where he falls in love with Miranda. Prospero takes Ferdinand prisoner to test his love for Miranda.
'Here is everything advantageous to life' Gonzalo II.1.48 *'While you here do snoring lie, Open-eye'd conspiracy His time doth take.'* Ariel II.1.295-7 *'I'll bear him no more sticks, but follow thee, Thou wondrous man.'* Caliban II.2.163-4	**Act II**	Antonio and Sebastian mock Gonzalo and blame Alonso for the 'loss' of Ferdinand. Gonzalo outlines his ideal 'commonwealth'. Antonio persuades Sebastian to murder the sleeping Alonso and Gonzalo so that Sebastian may become the king. Ariel saves Alonso and Gonzalo by waking them up. Caliban meets Stephano and Trinculo and decides to follow Stephano, believing he is a god.

Time	Action
Act III	

'O most dear mistress, The sun will set before I shall discharge What I must strive to do'

Ferdinand III.1.21-3

'Why, as I told thee, 'tis a custom with him I' th' afternoon to sleep: there thou mayst brain him, Having first seiz'd his books'

Caliban III.2.84-6

'You are three men of sin'

Ariel III.3.53

Act III

Ferdinand carries logs and promises to marry Miranda.

Caliban persuades Stephano and Trinculo to kill Prospero.

Ariel appears before Alonso etc and denounces the betrayal of Prospero.

Act IV

'Then, as my gift, and thine own acquisition Worthily purchas'd, take my daughter'

Prospero IV.1.13-14

'... the minute of their plot Is almost come'

Prospero IV.1.141-2

Prospero agrees that Ferdinand and Miranda can marry. A masque is performed.

Caliban, Stephano and Trinculo have been led into a bog by Ariel and are chased off by spirits.

Act V

6pm

'On the sixth hour; at which time, my lord, You said our work should cease'

Ariel V.1.4-5

'But this rough magic I here abjure'

Prospero V.1.50-1

Prospero reveals himself to Alonso etc in a magic circle and forgives them. Ferdinand and Miranda are revealed. Alonso restores Prospero's dukedom.

Prospero frees Ariel and renounces magic.

Stephano himself wants to rule it, he must first kill Prospero. Stephano resolves to do this and then make himself and Miranda king and queen of the island. Caliban leads Stephano and Trinculo to Prospero's cell.

Unable to find Ferdinand, Alonso and his court give him up for dead. They are confronted by some strange spirits who lay a banquet for them and invite them to eat. Just as they are about to eat, Ariel appears dressed as a harpy, and the banquet vanishes. The spirit denounces them for their crimes against Prospero, former Duke of Milan, and Alonso is immediately consumed with remorse. But Sebastian and Antonio, who are less touched by guilt, go off to fight the spirits.

Act IV   Prospero is satisfied that Ferdinand truly loves Miranda and agrees to their marriage; he warns Ferdinand not to have sex with her before the wedding. Ariel is summoned by Prospero to bring some spirits to perform a wedding **masque** (see Literary Terms), a magical trick which greatly impresses Ferdinand. Towards the end of the masque, Prospero remembers Caliban and his confederates, and their plot to kill him. Ariel has made them fall into a bog and when they get out they are filthy and wet. Prospero makes Ariel hang up some beautiful clothes outside his cell and as the would-be assassins attempt to put them on, other spirits in the shapes of dogs and hounds chase them off.

Act V   Finally, Prospero creates a magic circle into which step Alonso and his followers. In this charmed atmosphere, Gonzalo is praised for his kindness and loyalty and the others are forgiven for their crimes. Alonso gives Prospero back his dukedom and Prospero reveals that Ferdinand is alive. Ariel is freed and Caliban seeks forgiveness. The boatswain returns to tell them that the ship is completely seaworthy. In his last act of magic,

Prospero promises calm seas for their journey back to
Italy.

The play ends with Prospero renouncing his roles as a
magician and inviting the audience to applaud the
performance.

DETAILED SUMMARIES

ACT I

SCENE 1

*The shipwreck
provides a
dramatic opening
to the play.*

King Alonso of Naples and his court are voyaging
home from the wedding of his daughter in Tunisia,
when they are caught up in a fierce storm. While he is
working to save the ship, the boatswain is approached
by the royal party and he bluntly tells them to return to
their cabins because they are interfering with the work
of the sailors. The king's counsellor, Gonzalo, notes
that the boatswain has the appearance of the proverbial
man who is born to be hanged, not drowned, therefore
they should have nothing to fear.

*The audience's
interest in the fate
of the characters is
heightened when
they leap into the
sea.*

Antonio, Sebastian and Gonzalo return to the deck
after escorting Alonso to his cabin, and once gain the
boatswain rebukes them. Antonio and Sebastian curse
the boatswain for his insolence, but Gonzalo is more
tolerant of the man. The ship begins to break up so all
the passengers leap overboard.

COMMENT

This scene is a kind of prologue to the play and is the
only one not set on the island. It provides an initial
crisis and disruption which the rest of the play will
move to resolve.

The storm causes the conventional roles associated with
the characters' status to be reversed – the boatswain, a
normally low status character, orders the king and court
below deck and asks, lines 16–17, 'What cares these

Although a disaster is enacted, the scene does have some comic dimensions.

roarers for the name of the King?'. There will be several challenges to authority in the course of the play, thus the storm can be seen as a **metaphor** (see Literary Terms) for an important theme.

Gonzalo is shown to be an optimistic character in his reaction to the crisis, lines 28–30, and he is courteous to the blunt boatswain, whereas Sebastian and Antonio are abusive, lines 40–5. Later events will prove how morally inferior these two are to the decent and loyal Gonzalo.

Make a list of all the sea and nautical terms. There will be many references to the sea in the play.

Little scenery or elaborate stage effects would have been used in Shakespeare's theatre. The language creates vivid pictures of the storm for the audience's imagination to work on, and through the numerous authentic nautical terms employed by the boatswain.

GLOSSARY

you the boatswain shows deference to the nobility by using 'you' in spite of his bluntness

yarely quickly, smartly

roarers wind and waves

his complexion is perfect gallows his appearance indicates he was born to be hanged

the washing of ten tides in Elizabethan times pirates were left hanged on the shore until three tides had come in and gone out

SCENE 2

We discover that the storm was caused by Prospero's magic – his 'art'.

Through telling Miranda about her past, Prospero provides the audience with important information to prepare it for future events.

Prospero depicts himself as a virtuous man who has been badly wronged.

On the island, Miranda has been watching the shipwreck and she pleads with her father to ease the storm since it was his magical powers that started it. Prospero tells her she need not pity anyone who was on the ship for they will come to no harm; it was for her sake that he had used his magic. He then proceeds to tell her about her past, about which Miranda has only the vaguest memories. It is twelve years since Prospero, her father, was Duke of Milan, a man of great importance, but thanks to the treachery of his brother, Antonio, whom Prospero had trusted, he lost his dukedom. Prospero had been a great scholar and was more interested in study than in holding political power. Because of this he had entrusted Antonio with more and more responsibility for the government of the state, until his ambitious brother wanted to be the Duke of Milan himself. Antonio made a deal with Alonso, King of Naples. He offered to pay the king an annual tribute and make Milan subject to his authority if Alonso would help him depose Prospero. Alonso agreed and in the dead of night sent an army to take Prospero and Miranda out of Milan. They were afraid to kill them because Prospero was so greatly loved by the people, so they cast father and daughter adrift in an old boat without sails or tackle, hoping the pair would eventually die at sea. One thing, however, saved their lives: the kindness of 'a noble Neopolitan' called Gonzalo. This man had been put in charge of the plan to get rid of Prospero and he placed food, clothing, water and some of Prospero's beloved books in the boat. So they finally drifted to the island where Prospero has devoted himself to Miranda's care and education. It is very fortunate that Prospero's former enemies had been sailing near the island and by raising a storm he could bring them to its shores. This is an opportunity for justice to be done.

While Miranda is sleeping Prospero summons his
servant, the spirit Ariel, who tells him how he has
carried out Prospero's orders. He describes how he
stirred up the ocean and attacked the ship with
lightning bolts so that it burned like hell itself.
Everyone aboard, except the sailors, plunged into the
sea, but Ariel made sure they came to no harm – all
came ashore on different parts of the island and the
king's ship was safely harboured in a secret cove.

Ariel, like Caliban,   Ariel reminds Prospero of his promise to set him free.
longs for freedom.   He thinks that after all his labours on Prospero's behalf,
he should now be given his liberty. But the indignant
Prospero declines to do this and reminds Ariel of 'the
foul witch Sycorax'. She had been banished to the
island from Algeria. Ariel had been her servant but had
refused to perform her commands; for this he was
imprisoned in a pine tree and had remained there for
twelve years, during which time Sycorax died, leaving
the only other inhabitant of the island, her son,
Caliban. It was Prospero's magic that set Ariel free; if
the spirit complains again, warns Prospero, he will find
himself imprisoned in an oak tree. Ariel promises to
continue to obey Prospero's commands and is told that
he will be set free in two days.

After Ariel has gone, Prospero wakes up Miranda,
telling her that they are going to visit Caliban. Miranda
cannot stand the sight of this 'villain' and is reluctant to
go, but Prospero tells her that Caliban is their servant
and cannot be avoided. He calls the creature from out
of his den and while they are waiting for him, Ariel
returns disguised as a water-nymph to receive more
instructions from Prospero.

Both Caliban and   When Caliban appears he curses Prospero and Miranda
Ariel resent their   bemoaning the way Prospero took the island from him
enslavement to   and turned him into a slave. He reminds Prospero of
Prospero.   how he loved him at first, showing him all the good

things of the place in return for Prospero's seemingly
kind interest in him. When he had first come to the
island Prospero had taught Caliban many things and
even let him live with himself and Miranda in his cell,
but Caliban had tried to rape the girl. Caliban is
unrepentant and says he wishes that he had managed to
father several Calibans from Miranda. However, he
realises he must obey Prospero, for the old man
commands the power of magic and will punish him
severely if he does not.

Ferdinand and
Miranda fall in
love through the
power of
Prospero's magic.

An invisible Ariel, playing and singing, lures Ferdinand
to Prospero's cell where he first sees Miranda and they
fall instantly in love. Prospero is secretly delighted
because this was his intention. But first he decides to
put Ferdinand through some hardship to test the
strength of his love for Miranda. He uses his magic
powers to disarm the young man and takes him
prisoner. Ferdinand resolves that, in spite of all the
suffering he has endured that day, if he can still see
Miranda even at a distance, then imprisonment will be
bearable. Miranda reassures Ferdinand that her father is
a better man than he appears; Prospero, for his part, has
more plans for Ariel to carry out.

COMMENT

In this scene we are introduced to all the inhabitants
of the island and learn about their past and their
relationship to each other:
* When he tells Miranda about Antonio's treachery,
  lines 66–87, Prospero's language becomes convoluted
  and disjointed under the pressure of his emotions. He
  was a very important man and his fall from power
  provides the main impulse for the action of the play.
* Many aspects of Prospero's complex character are
  revealed in this long scene, not least the fact that he
  controls everything that happens. Now that his
  enemies are on the island will he use this power for
  justice or revenge?

*Original
performances of the
play would probably
have taken place in
the afternoon.*

*Two kinds of
magic: black and
white.*

- Prospero's authority is challenged by both Ariel and Caliban, thus continuing the theme introduced by the boatswain in Scene 1 and implicit in Prospero's account of how he lost his dukedom.
- Although he was betrayed by Antonio, Prospero lost his dukedom partly because he preferred secretive studies which were beyond the people's understanding, lines 89–97, thus neglecting his duties as a ruler. This situation awoke his brother's 'evil nature'.
- The action of *The Tempest* covers about four hours – a single afternoon, lines 238–41. In this it almost conforms to the classical unity (see Literary Terms) of time, which dictates that the timespan covered by the action of the play should correspond to the performance time.
- The story of the witch, Sycorax, parallels that of Prospero. Both are exiled on the island, both have a child, both practise magic, and both use Ariel as a servant. But the latter, in refusing to perform 'her earthy and abhorr'd commands' (line 273) is made ready for the service of a far more superior magic than that practised by the 'malignant' Sycorax. Furthermore, the moral inferiority of Sycorax and Caliban is reflected in their physical ugliness, deformity in Shakespeare's time being considered a sign of parental wickedness. Miranda, needless to say, is beautiful and therefore good.
- We meet Caliban and learn his version of the events which led to his enslavement, lines 333–46. He is resentful of Prospero – 'This island's mine' – and how much sympathy the audience has with him depends on how his character is interpreted. Is he a brutal inhuman monster, or an exploited savage?
- The way Miranda and Ferdinand are made to fall in love by Prospero's magic art introduces an element of romantic fairy tale to the play. Combined with the

formal language of Prospero – 'The fringed curtains of thine eye advance' (line 411) – this produces an artificial effect which is not intended to be received as realistic. Shakespeare is dramatising the idea of love and its power to alleviate suffering.

GLOSSARY   **welkin** sky

amazement terror

virtue essence

bootless inquisition pointless questioning

a piece of virtue perfect example of virtuous womanhood

teen troubles

signories dukedoms

trach for over-topping check because he was becoming too ambitious

undergoing stomach courage, fortitude

steaded much helped a lot

coil tumult

at least two glasses at least two o'clock

hests commands

control contradict

my foot my tutor? shall I be instructed by an inferior?

A *Identify the speaker.*

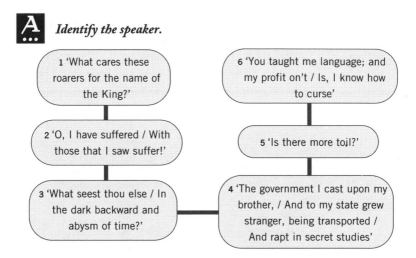

1 'What cares these roarers for the name of the King?'

2 'O, I have suffered / With those that I saw suffer!'

3 'What seest thou else / In the dark backward and abysm of time?'

6 'You taught me language; and my profit on't / Is, I know how to curse'

5 'Is there more toil?'

4 'The government I cast upon my brother, / And to my state grew stranger, being transported / And rapt in secret studies'

Identify the person 'to whom' this comment refers.

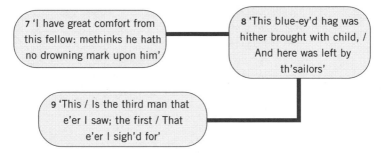

7 'I have great comfort from this fellow: methinks he hath no drowning mark upon him'

8 'This blue-ey'd hag was hither brought with child, / And here was left by th'sailors'

9 'This / Is the third man that e'er I saw; the first / That e'er I sigh'd for'

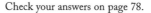

Check your answers on page 78.

B *Consider these issues.*

a How authority is challenged at the beginning of the play.

b The idea of the storm and shipwreck as a **metaphor** (see Literary Terms).

c Prospero's motives and how they relate to his past.

d The function of magic in the play.

e Caliban's attitude to Prospero, and how he came to be upon the island.

f The way Miranda and Ferdinand are made to fall in love.

ACT II

SCENE 1

*The cynical
Antonio and
Sebastian are
incapable of seeing
any goodness in
Gonzalo's
'commonwealth'.*

Alonso and his followers are wandering about on another part of the island, searching for Ferdinand, King Alonso's son. Gonzalo's attempts to comfort his king are rejected by Alonso and mocked by Antonio and Sebastian. Taking a rational view of their predicament, Gonzalo believes they should be grateful to have escaped unharmed and arrived in such a fine place where 'everything [is] advantageous to life' (line 48). The despairing Alonso, who believes his son Ferdinand is dead, regrets marrying his daughter to the King of Tunisia because in doing so he has lost both his heirs. Sebastian is quick to blame him for this, but Gonzalo suggests that the island could be the site of an ideal state, a 'commonwealth' in which everyone would equally share the goodness of nature. The old man's views weary the king and Antonio and Sebastian ridicule his idealism.

Ariel arrives, invisible and playing music. He causes Alonso, Gonzalo, Francisco and Adrian to fall asleep, during which time Antonio persuades Sebastian that this is his chance to become King of Naples. He could do what Antonio did to become Duke of Milan: kill his brother and seize the power for himself. Sebastian agrees and promises that after Alonso is dead he will release Antonio from his obligation of the tribute which Milan pays to Naples. But Prospero has foreseen this danger. His invisible servant, Ariel, sings in Gonzalo's ear just as the would-be assassins are about to strike. The courtier wakes up and rouses Alonso who demands to know why Antonio and Sebastian have their swords drawn. They pretend that they had heard the roaring of wild animals and were making ready to protect their sleeping companions. This explanation satisfies

Alonso and Gonzalo, and the party resume the search for Ferdinand.

COMMENT

Francisco provides a vivid picture of Ferdinand swimming ashore.

We discover how much King Alonso loves his son, Ferdinand, and how deeply he grieves for him, lines 107–9. The king's courtiers are divided between those who try to comfort him and those who are unsympathetic.

Antonio and Sebastian deploy **puns** (see Literary Terms) in their malicious mockery of Gonzalo. Such witty playing with language is characteristic of Shakespeare's work generally. Here, it draws attention to the characters of Antonio and Sebastian. Although they appear to be cleverer than Gonzalo, they lack his vision and imaginative willingness to adapt to a new situation. Their puns would go down well in a royal court; on the island they make Antonio and Sebastian look hollow and limited.

Gonzalo reveals that the royal party was returning home from the marriage of Claribel, Alonso's daughter, to the King of Tunis.

The unsophisticated Gonzalo does not appreciate the implications of comparing Claribel to the mythical 'widow' Dido, Queen of Carthage. In Virgil's *Aeneid* she had an affair with Aeneas, the Trojan Prince, and committed suicide after he abandoned her. She was a widow, but was not often referred to as such. Gonzalo also mistakes Tunis for Carthage (line 80).

Sebastian is critical of Alonso, lines 118–30. He blames all their misfortune on Alonso's determination to marry Claribel to an 'African', when all the court begged him not to. He does not care about his brother's grief, but maliciously attempts to increase his suffering. This prepares the audience for his readiness to let Antonio kill Alonso later in the scene.

In contrast to the malice and cynicism of Antonio and Sebastian, Gonzalo attempts to comfort the king by outlining what he would do if he were the king on an island. Gonzalo's 'commonwealth', lines 143–60, is a description of an ideal society derived by Shakespeare from an essay, *On Cannibals*, written by the French philosopher, Michel de Montaigne (1533–92).

Antonio and Sebastian both betray their respective brothers. Antonio encourages Sebastian to seize Alonso's throne in a way which is worth comparing with the great temptation scenes in *Macbeth*, Act I Scenes 5 and 7. First, he challenges him to be active and offers to show him what to do, 'I'll teach you how to flow' (line 217). Then he gets him to admit that Ferdinand must be dead (line 227) by discrediting the comfort offered to the king by Gonzalo. He appeals to Sebastian's 'ambition' and asserts that the real heir to the throne, Claribel, now lives too far from Naples. He uses exaggerated language (**hyperbole** – see Literary Terms), 'beyond man's life' (line 241), and theatrical **imagery** (see Literary Terms), 'And by that destiny, to perform an act / Whereof what's past is prologue' (lines 246–7) – all of which is designed to act on Sebastian's emotions.

Antonio sees lack of conscience as a kind of virtue. Antonio finally secures Sebastian's agreement by offering himself as a role model. He had no conscience about supplanting his own brother, Prospero, and has never been troubled by what he did – 'I feel not / This deity in my bosom' (lines 272–3). If they kill Gonzalo as well, Alonso's other followers will easily submit to them. The ruthless way he has drawn out Sebastian's ambition is ultimately reflected in Antonio's willingness to kill Alonso himself. Perhaps his shrewd political mind sees this as a way of putting Sebastian in his debt when he is king.

Antonio uses vivid images when he tells Sebastian his plan, lines 271–85. The mixture of **personification,**

metaphor and simile (see Literary Terms) contrasts
with Sebastian's literal response, lines 285–9. This
indirect mode of expression partly reflects Antonio's
deviousness, his ability to use language for an evil
purpose.

GLOSSARY

visitor someone who visits the sick

Temperance was a delicate wench a girl's name often use by the
Puritans

As many vouch'd rarities are many strange occurrences may be
guaranteed as true and yet are almost beyond belief

He hath rais'd the wall Antonio and Sebastian compare
Gonzalo to Amphion, King of Thebes, who rose the walls
of the city when he played his harp. By mistaking Tunis for
Carthage, Gonzalo has raised a whole city merely by his
words

Who hath cause to wet the grief on't you who have good cause to
grieve over this grievous situation

chirurgeonly surgeon-like

plantation colonisation – deliberately misinterpreted by
Sebastian and Antonio to mean 'planting'

Letters education

succession inheritance of land, property, wealth

Save God save

sphere the orbit of the moon around the earth was known as its
sphere in Ptolemaic astronomy

hereditary sloth natural laziness, having been born after my
brother

chough as of deep chat a bird could talk as sensibly as he
does

'Twould put me to slipper it would make me wear slippers

SCENE 2

*In this scene
Shakespeare focuses
attention on
Caliban.*

Caliban is carrying logs for Prospero. He curses his
master for sending spirits to torture him. He sees
Trinculo, King Alonso's jester, approaching and
believes he is one of Prospero's spirits come to torment
him. He lies down to hide. A storm is brewing and

Corrupt early settlers exploited Indians by pretending to be gods.

Trinculo, looking for somewhere to shelter, sees Caliban. He decides to hide from the rain under the cloak of this strange 'fish' (line 25). Stephano, Alonso's butler, appears. He is drinking wine from a bottle and sings a song. Then he notices Caliban's cloak with four legs sticking out of it and believes he has come across some kind of monster. Caliban, who thinks Stephano is also one of Prospero's spirits, begs not to be tormented. Stephano gives Caliban some drink and is amazed to find Trinculo under the cloak. This is Caliban's first taste of alcohol and he is convinced that Stephano must be some kind of god to give him such 'celestial liquor' (line 118). He resolves to leave Prospero's service and follow Stephano, promising to show his new-found friends all the good things on the island. Singing drunkenly, Caliban leads them off.

COMMENT   Two new characters are introduced and a comic **sub-plot** (see Literary Terms) is begun.

Both Trinculo and Stephano think of ways they could exploit the 'monster' Caliban for profit, lines 28–34 and 69–72. In Elizabethan and Jacobean times it was common to see Indians exhibited as freaks in public places. Many of them died from this experience, hence 'dead Indian' (line 34).

Shakespeare's attitude towards this practice, and to other aspects of colonialism in general, may be critical. Trinculo's remark, lines 32–4, about the uncharitable public certainly has a sardonic sting which the original audience would have noted.

Compare Caliban's language (lines 160–4) to that of the other two.

Caliban's willingness to serve Stephano and show him the natural riches of the island echoes his relationship to Prospero when he first came to the island.

Trinculo is persistently contemptuous of Caliban, repeatedly calling him 'monster' (line 144 onwards). Neither he nor Stephano see Caliban as a person, but as a thing to be used. Trinculo dislikes and fears Caliban.

Caliban's drunken cry of 'freedom' (lines 186–7) at the end of the scene is ironic; he has merely become another master's slave.

Stephano's remark ('The King and all our company else being drown'd, we will inherit here' – lines 174–5) reflects the issue of rightful inheritance and possession of authority which features in the main plot.

GLOSSARY

inch-meal bit by bit

mow grimace

bombard a large leather vessel

Poor-John a fish

make a man make a man's fortune

doit a small coin

neat's-leather cowhide

siege excrement

butt of sack barrel of wine

crabs crab apples

scamel a sea bird

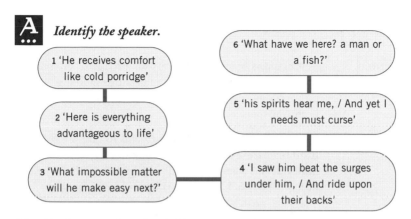

A *Identify the speaker.*

1 'He receives comfort like cold porridge'

2 'Here is everything advantageous to life'

3 'What impossible matter will he make easy next?'

6 'What have we here? a man or a fish?'

5 'his spirits hear me, / And yet I needs must curse'

4 'I saw him beat the surges under him, / And ride upon their backs'

Identify the person 'to whom' this comment refers.

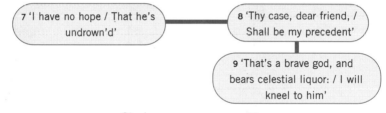

7 'I have no hope / That he's undrown'd'

8 'Thy case, dear friend, / Shall be my precedent'

9 'That's a brave god, and bears celestial liquor: / I will kneel to him'

Check your answers on page 78.

B *Consider these issues.*

a How the shipwrecked court becomes divided into separate groups, each with its own agenda.

b Gonzalo's 'commonwealth' is an attractive vision of what society could become. But in many ways it is an unrealistic example of naive idealism. Reflect on how far we are meant to see it in relation to Gonzalo's character.

c The way Antonio draws out Sebastian's ambition to be king.

d Antonio and Sebastian are 'civilised', intelligent, highly educated Europeans, yet they are prepared to perform an evil action. In depicting them like this, and then showing how other members of the court behave when they meet Caliban, consider how far Shakespeare may be criticising contemporary colonialism.

ACT III

SCENE 1

Ferdinand is seen carrying logs for Prospero. He reflects on how thinking of Miranda makes this labour a pleasure, and then Miranda herself appears. Unseen by both, Prospero observes them.

Miranda tries to persuade Ferdinand to take some rest from his hard work, and she offers to carry logs for him, but the young man will not let her do this – he'd rather break his back than sit by and watch such a 'precious creature' (line 25) work.

Soon they are confessing their love for one another and Miranda tells him that she will marry him. After they have left the stage, Prospero expresses great pleasure in the love that has grown between his daughter and the son of the King of Naples.

COMMENT

The purpose of this short scene is to establish the relationship of Miranda and Ferdinand.

The physical presence of Prospero on the stage, unknown to the couple, emphasises his role as the controller of events.

Ferdinand is forced to do the same sort of work as Caliban. Unlike Caliban, however, he alleviates his labours with 'sweet thoughts' (line 14) of Miranda.

Miranda speaks indirectly of her feelings at first, then decides to plainly tell Ferdinand that she will be his wife if he wants her, lines 77–83. When Miranda refers to her way of speaking in **riddles** (see Literary Terms) she uses an image of fertility, 'the more it seeks to hide itself, / The bigger bulk it shows' (lines 80–1), which connects with the **imagery** of the **masque** (see Literary Terms) in Act IV.

GLOSSARY   **quickens** brings to life

sore injunctions an order that will be severely punished if it is disobeyed

Most busilest when I do it [these thoughts] are most active when I am working

Visitation visit (also used of a plague epidemic)

put it to the foil show unfavourably

invert what best is boded me to mischief convert whatever good fortune I may have to evil

follow companion

As bondage e'er of freedom as such as a slave desires freedom

A thousand thousand! a thousand farewells

appertaining relating to my plans

SCENE 2

This scene resumes the activities of Caliban, Stephano and Trinculo. They are getting drunk and Trinculo is continuing to be contemptuous of Caliban. Ariel enters, invisible to the other three, and imitates Trinculo's voice. He calls Caliban a liar when Caliban tells *Caliban believes*   Stephano about Prospero's 'cunning' sorcery. Stephano *the island*   tells Trinculo to leave Caliban alone and beats him *belonged to him*   when Ariel calls him a liar too. Trinculo blames *before Prospero*   their behaviour on the amount of wine they have *usurped it.*   consumed.

Another conspiracy Caliban continues to tell Stephano about Prospero. He
begins. says that Prospero has no power without his books, so if
Stephano seizes them he will be able to kill Prospero
while he is having his afternoon nap. Caliban tells
Stephano about the beautiful Miranda and Stephano
decides to kill Prospero and become king of the island;
Miranda will be his queen. Ariel causes further
confusion when he plays the tune of their song on a
pipe, but Caliban reassures Stephano and Trinculo that
this mysterious music is often heard on the island.
Stephano and Trinculo follow Caliban off the stage.

COMMENT Trinculo can hold his liquor better than his companions
and has a clearer view of what is going on. His
comments are argumentative and critical. Note the
number of **puns** (see Literary Terms) he employs, a
style of speech typical of a court jester.

The scene provides a comic contrast to the previous
scene featuring Miranda and Ferdinand. The action
reflects one of the main themes of the play (i.e. the
wrongful assumption of authority) in the form of a
parody (see Literary Terms):
- Stephano starts behaving like a king and demands
  obedience from his 'subjects', Caliban and Trinculo.
- Caliban's plan to kill Prospero parallels Antonio and
  Sebastian's plot to murder Alonso in his sleep.
- Caliban's plan also reflects elements of the original
  plot against Prospero when he was Duke of Milan:
  Stephano is told to burn Prospero's books, which are
  the source of his power and which are part of the
  cause of his overthrow.

Ironically, although Caliban is a savage, he speaks some
of the most beautifully poetic lines in the play, lines
133–41. This must qualify our view of his character,
which is not as straightforwardly brutal as his 'savage
and deformed' role implies. Caliban is meant to be seen

as uncivilised, yet his feelings for the beauty of the island have genuine sensitivity (see also I.2.334–40).

(see also I.2.334–40)

GLOSSARY

bear up and board 'em drink up
standard standard bearer
debosh'd debauched
pied ninny multicoloured fool
quick freshes quick-flowing springs
murrain plague
wezand windpipe
cout make a fool of
scout sneer
by the picture of Nobody by an invisible person
take't as thou list take whatever shape you like

SCENE 3

On another part of the island, a weary Alonso and his followers pause in their search for Ferdinand. Antonio and Sebastian are still conspiring to kill the king. They decide that a good opportunity would be that very night, when Alonso and Gonzalo will be exhausted by their travels and therefore less watchful than before.

In Greek mythology a 'harpy' had a woman's face and body but the wings and claws of a bird.

Prospero appears. To the sound of strange music, some of his spirits lay a feast before the royal party and invite them to eat. When the spirits leave, they decide to eat the food, but before they can do so, Ariel appears dressed as a harpy. He reminds Alonso, Antonio and Sebastian of their wickedness towards Prospero and his innocent child. Ariel and then the banquet disappear. Prospero reflects that he now has his enemies in his power and then leaves, unseen by the others. Alonso is full of remorse at the wrong he has done to Prospero. Antonio and Sebastian, though, resolve to fight the spirits and go off to find them.

Prospero has arranged the apparition to produce a particular effect upon the king.

COMMENT

The expressions of amazement uttered by the court when they see the spirits gives us some insight into the tales brought back by travellers in Shakespeare's day,

Ariel's accusation has a powerful effect on Alonso. and the reception they received at home. There are references to mythical figures, the unicorn and the phoenix, and to people similar to those referred to by Walter Raleigh in his writings on Guiana (1596): 'of people whose heads appear not above their shoulders ... they are reported to have their eyes in their shoulders, and their mouths in the middle of their breasts'.

The presence of Prospero on the stage, unseen by all the others, yet controlling the events, again emphasises the God-like role he is playing.

Gonzalo does not hear Ariel's words, lines 53–82, and therefore believes that the strange behaviour of Alonso, Antonio and Sebastian is caused by 'their great guilt' (line 104), which has been working on them from within like a slow poison. Only Alonso is able to feel his guilt; he thinks he has been accused of his wrongdoing by Nature itself (lines 96–9).

GLOSSARY

By'r lakin 'Ladykin' – the Virgin Mary

maze a garden with winding paths designed as a puzzle. Here it might also symbolise the moral journey of King Alonso

drollery puppet show

unicorn a mythical horse with one horn on its forehead

phoenix mythical bird. It was the only one of its kind. It built its own funeral pyre and after death rose from the ashes

muse wonder at

dew-lapped skin hanging from the throats of cows and bulls

Each putter-out of five for one each underwriter who had taken a traveller's deposit before departure and promised to repay the sum fivefold on return

dowle small feather

stare roar

bass my trespass sing my sin in a loud, low voice

ecstasy madness

A *Identify the speaker.*

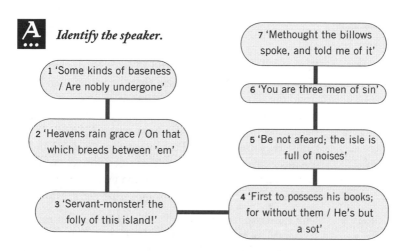

1 'Some kinds of baseness / Are nobly undergone'

2 'Heavens rain grace / On that which breeds between 'em'

3 'Servant-monster! the folly of this island!'

7 'Methought the billows spoke, and told me of it'

6 'You are three men of sin'

5 'Be not afeard; the isle is full of noises'

4 'First to possess his books; for without them / He's but a sot'

Identify the person 'to whom' this comment refers.

8 'If you'll sit down, / I'll bear your logs the while'

9 'Let me lick thy shoe'

10 'I am right glad that he's so out of hope'

Check your answers on page 78.

B *Consider these issues.*

a Why Miranda quickly offers to marry Ferdinand (III.1.83–5) even though he is the first man she has ever met besides her father.

b Normally, low-status characters such as Caliban speak in **prose** (see Literary Terms) in Shakespeare's plays. Perhaps there is a reason why Caliban has been given some memorably poetic lines in Scene 2, lines 133–41.

c The way the comic **sub-plot** (see Literary Terms) featuring Caliban, Stephano and Trinculo parodies certain aspects of the main plot.

d The reaction of the court to Prospero's spirits.

e How Prospero makes Alonso, Antonio and Sebastian confront their former sins.

f Why Alonso is full of guilt at the end of the Act, but Antonio and Sebastian only feel hostility.

ACT IV

SCENE 1

Prospero warns the couple against pre-marital intercourse twice. Chastity was highly valued in Jacobean times.

The elaborate masque emphasises the symbolic significance of the couple's betrothal.

Is Prospero right to think that Caliban is 'a born devil'?

Prospero returns to his cell and releases Ferdinand from his punishment. He is pleased that the young man has stood the test of his love for Miranda and agrees to let them marry, though Prospero is careful to warn Ferdinand not to have intercourse with Miranda before they are married. Prospero summons Ariel and instructs him to bring the spirits to perform a **masque** (see Literary Terms) to celebrate the betrothal of the couple.

The spirits appear in the guise of Greek Goddesses: Iris, goddess of the rainbow; Juno, queen of the gods; Ceres, goddess of fertility. At the end, naiads, spirits of the waters, appear and dance with a group of reapers. During the performance of the masque, Ferdinand expresses great pleasure in this poetic spectacle, and admiration for the magic skill of Prospero. But the latter brings the masque to an abrupt end when he remembers that Caliban, Stephano and Trinculo are planning to kill him. He asks Ferdinand to forgive his sudden change of mood and, after sending the young couple into his cell, he summons Ariel.

Ariel recounts to Prospero how he charmed the three drunken conspirators with his music and led them into a stagnant pool, where he left them up to their chins in foul-smelling water. Prospero tells Ariel to go and hang up some fine-looking garments on a line outside his cell; with these he intends to distract the three plotters from their goal. Prospero and Ariel then make themselves invisible so that they can observe Caliban, Stephano and Trinculo when they arrive.

Soon the plotters come in, soaked to the skin and filthy. Stephano and Trinculo are very disgruntled and

Caliban thinks Stephano and Trinculo are fools.

blame Caliban for the trick that has been played on them, especially since they have lost their wine in the pool. Caliban becomes impatient with the two men when they start quarrelling over who should wear the clothes: he tells them that the clothes are 'trash' and urges them to stick to their plan to murder Prospero. Stephano and Trinculo, however, dismiss Caliban's advice and become preoccupied with the clothes. At this point, Prospero and Ariel release their spirits in the shape of hounds which chase the plotters away.

COMMENT

Ferdinand uses a conventional figure for male sexual desire when he tells Prospero that his emotions are under control, line 30. The idea is alluded to shortly after by Prospero: 'do not give dalliance / Too much the rein' (lines 51–2).

Prospero's insistence on the importance of chastity is taken up in the **masque** (see Literary Terms) when Iris assures Ceres that Venus, goddess of love, and her son Cupid, will not be taking part in the celebration (lines 91–101).

Masques were popular entertainment at the courts of Queen Elizabeth and King James I. They had lavish costumes, elaborate devices were employed to create unusual scenic effects, and they always incorporated

Note the different stages of the masque. stylised poetic dialogue, music and dancing. Masques almost invariably dealt with classical or mythological subjects, in which gods and goddesses, **personifications** (see Literary Terms) of abstract qualities, such as Grace and Hope, performed a series of events usually in celebration of marriage. The masque in Act IV is a typical example. Its theme is the abundant fruitfulness of the natural world.

Prospero's speech to Ferdinand, lines 148–58, has an elegiac quality in keeping with the spirit of Shakespeare's last play. The speech moves from the specific theatrical **imagery** (see Literary Terms) of the 'pageant' to a general reflection on the impermanence of human existence.

Prospero encapsulates an important theme of the play, lines 188–90. He has been unable to educate Caliban in the civilised values of his aristocratic class, whereas Miranda, whose nature is superior, has benefited from Prospero's nurture (see I.2.171–4).

Ironically, Stephano and Trinculo end up looking more foolish than the 'monster' Caliban. Their ludicrous posturing in the flashy garments shows how easily they have been taken in by appearances, and Caliban knows the consequences of this only too well, lines 231–4.

GLOSSARY   **aspersion** blessing
Hymen Greek god of marriage
worser genius bad angel
Phoebus god of the sun, who drove his chariot around the skies
vanity trivial illusion, trick
liver the source of physical desire
pioned and twilled dug and woven
bosky wooded

dusky Dis the dark god of the underworld

hot minion passionate lover

trumpery flashy clothes

hoodwink this mischance make compensation for this misfortune

line clothes line and equinoctial line

lose your hair Stephano is referring to the belief that people lost
their hair when they crossed the equator

pass of pate witty remark

A Identify the speaker.

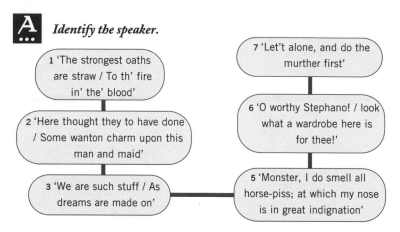

1 'The strongest oaths are straw / To th' fire in' the' blood'

2 'Here thought they to have done / Some wanton charm upon this man and maid'

3 'We are such stuff / As dreams are made on'

5 'Monster, I do smell all horse-piss; at which my nose is in great indignation'

6 'O worthy Stephano! / look what a wardrobe here is for thee!'

7 'Let't alone, and do the murther first'

Identify the person 'to whom' this comment refers.

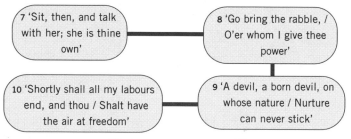

7 'Sit, then, and talk with her; she is thine own'

8 'Go bring the rabble, / O'er whom I give thee power'

9 'A devil, a born devil, on whose nature / Nurture can never stick'

10 'Shortly shall all my labours end, and thou / Shalt have the air at freedom'

Check your answers on page 78.

B Consider these issues.

a The way Prospero 'hands over' Miranda to Ferdinand.

b Why Prospero twice warns Ferdinand not to have sexual intercourse with Miranda.

c Why Prospero is so troubled by Caliban's plot to murder him.

d Prospero's conception of 'nurture' and whether he is right to call Caliban a 'born devil'.

e The **symbolism** (see Literary Terms) of the 'glistering apparel' when worn by 'King Stephano'.

f How Caliban feels towards Stephano and Trinculo at the end of this Act.

ACT V

SCENE 1

Prospero affirms his humanity by deciding to forgive his enemies.

The time has arrived when Prospero's plans are to come to fruition. He instructs Ariel to bring the royal party to his cell. Alonso, Sebastian and Antonio have been kept spell-bound behind some trees nearby, while Gonzalo and the other courtiers have been unable to do anything for them. Prospero decides to break the power of the spell and forgive his enemies.

Some commentators have interpreted lines 33–57 as Shakespeare's farewell to play-writing.

Note that neither Sebastian nor Antonio speak much in this scene. Do they feel genuine remorse?

Ariel leads the royal party in and they enter a circle which Prospero has prepared for them. Alonso, Sebastian and Antonio are in a distracted state, but after a while the effects of the spell wear off and they regain their normal state of mind. Prospero reveals himself to the royal party, rebukes Alonso, Sebastian and Antonio for their crimes before he forgives them, and then thanks Gonzalo for his loyalty and kindness. The unhappy Alonso, who still believes Ferdinand is dead, is overjoyed to discover that his son is not only alive, but is to marry Prospero's daughter, Miranda.

The ship's master and the boatswain are brought in by Ariel and they inform the king that his ship is miraculously preserved.

Ariel then brings in the three conspirators, all dressed in the stolen clothes. Stephano and Trinculo are reproved by Alonso. Caliban asks for forgiveness and admits that he has been a fool 'to take this drunkard for a god' (line 296).

Prospero announces that he will return to Naples with the royal party for the wedding of Ferdinand and Miranda, after which he will go back to Milan as its rightful duke. He invites the party to spend the night with him in his cell and to hear the strange story of his life on the island. For his final service to Prospero, Ariel is ordered to ensure that there will be good weather for their voyage back to Italy.

COMMENT Prospero's use of the word 'project' (line 1) implies the alchemist's experiment in which metal was turned into gold.

Prospero's project has several different yet related elements.

Prospero explains his reasons for showing forgiveness to his enemies, lines 20–30. Though his desire for revenge is strong, 'fury', he is ruled by his 'nobler reason' which prompts him to act with 'virtue'. The word has several connotations, such as chastity, mercy, or Christian love, and at this point in the play it demonstrates Prospero's essential nobility.

Prospero makes himself visible to the royal party, line 106, in a very theatrical manner, just after Gonzalo has appealed for a 'heavenly power' (line 105) to guide them out of their fearful situation. His first words, 'Behold, sir King' (line 107), seem to ironically allude to the god-like role he has played throughout the play.

Alonso's reaction to the appearance of Prospero, lines 111–19, is based on three elements: recognition of Prospero as the rightful Duke of Milan, realisation that his wrong-doing has been a 'madness' (line 116), and an immediate appeal for forgiveness.

Although he forgives Antonio and Sebastian, Prospero's language, lines 126–32, suggests a barely suppressed violence towards them.

For Christians 'loss' precedes salvation through knowledge of God.

Shakespeare makes Prospero and Alonso play on the word 'loss' (lines 137–52) to prepare the bond which will be established between them by the marriage of Ferdinand and Miranda. The word has strong thematic implications in the play as a whole, since Alonso and his court have lost their way both literally and morally. Gonzalo, at lines 208–13, underlines what has been 'found', and learned, from the interrupted voyage, thus indicating the restoration of rightful order at the end of the play.

At the time, chess was an aristocratic game where the sexes met on equal terms.

Miranda's comment, lines 183–4, when she encounters the royal court for the first time, is a fine example of **dramatic irony** (see Literary Terms). She is not aware, as the audience is, that 'beauteous mankind' includes those who have been shown to be morally degenerate.

When Prospero acknowledges that Caliban belongs to him, lines 275–6, he could also be admitting to a wicked aspect in his own nature. Equally, 'darkness' might simply refer to the colour of Caliban's skin.

Prospero remains in role to speak the Epilogue, which combines the actor's conventional appeal for the audience's indulgence with the idea of the magician who has forsaken magic.

GLOSSARY   **relish** feel
kindlier more humanly, generously
green sour ringlets a ring of poisonous toadstools
boiled over-excited
ev'n sociable to in fully sympathy with

remorse and nature pity and natural feelings
reasonable shore the mind
sometime Milan formerly Duke of Milan
An if this be at all if this actually happened and not an illusion
subtleties sweet confections
tricksy agile, inventive
was ever conduct of ever caused
infest your mind with beating worry your mind
shortly single soon privately
reeling ripe very drunk
fly-blowing Trinculo is like pickled meat, so cannot be
  contaminated by flies

A Identify the speaker.

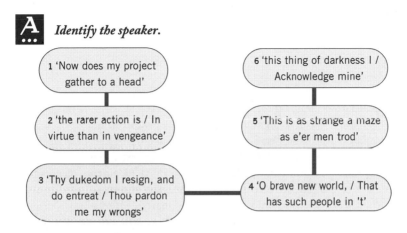

1 'Now does my project gather to a head'

6 'this thing of darkness I / Acknowledge mine'

2 'the rarer action is / In virtue than in vengeance'

5 'This is as strange a maze as e'er men trod'

3 'Thy dukedom I resign, and do entreat / Thou pardon me my wrongs'

4 'O brave new world, / That has such people in 't'

Identify the person 'to whom' this comment refers.

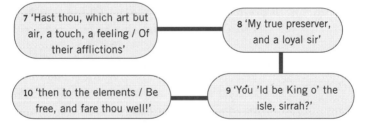

7 'Hast thou, which art but air, a touch, a feeling / Of their afflictions'

8 'My true preserver, and a loyal sir'

10 'then to the elements / Be free, and fare thou well!'

9 'You 'Id be King o' the isle, sirrah?'

Check your answers on page 78.

B Consider these issues.

a Why Prospero chooses to forgive his enemies.

b Why Prospero decides to forsake his 'rough magic'.

c The way Prospero forgives Antonio and Sebastian and why they do not express any remorse in the scene.

d The significance of the proposed marriage between Ferdinand and Miranda.

e The way Shakespeare shows how several of the characters have been taken in by 'appearances'.

f What Caliban is thinking when he utters his last words in the play.

PART THREE

COMMENTARY

THEMES

The Tempest *is Shakespeare's last play and reflects the ideas which preoccupied him at the end of his life.*

The Tempest is a richly complex play and consequently can be interpreted in many different ways. It has been seen as an autobiographical work, in which Shakespeare, through the character of Prospero, is marking the end of his life as an artist. Some commentators have focused on the elements of **masque** (see Literary Terms) in the play, and interpreted it as a celebration of a virtuous monarch. Others have responded to it as an example of the romance **genre** (see Literary Terms), with its characteristic mixture of fantastic improbabilities, love, magic and miraculous reconciliations. There are political, Christian and ethical issues in the play, which have attracted a wide range of interpretations also. However, when reading *The Tempest* for the first time it is unnecessary to think of it in terms of any fixed interpretative framework. The play contains some fundamental themes which, when identified, form the basis of a useful understanding for examination purposes.

NATURE OR NURTURE?

> A devil, a born devil, on whose nature
> Nurture can never stick (IV.1.188–9)

Two very different views of nature are developed in the play, views that were of great interest to educated Jacobeans at a time of colonial expansion in the New World. On the one hand, there is the view voiced by Gonzalo, Act II Scene 1, that the natural world is essentially good and that people living together without laws, customs, rulers or individual property would exist harmoniously and peacefully, provided for by nature's infinite abundance. This view derives from Montaigne's essay *Of Cannibals* which Shakespeare almost certainly knew and which implies that attempts by 'civilised' societies to educate the native inhabitants of the New World ran the risk of corrupting them. It lies behind Caliban's outburst in Act I Scene 2, 'You taught me language; and my profit on't is, I know how to curse' (line 365) and behind his lyrical descriptions of the 'qualities' of the island, which belonged entirely to him before Prospero arrived.

The nature/ nurture division is represented by the characters of Caliban and Miranda.

On the other hand, the second view of the natural world is that civilised man has a duty to control, educate and master nature because, left to itself, it will do only evil. The values of civilisation, or 'nurture', are represented by Prospero, and his failure to educate Caliban, who is guided by his 'natural' lusts, greed, envy and violence, is an indication of the wide gap that exists between the civilised, morally superior being and the savage.

But Shakespeare's genius is such that neither of these viewpoints is given without qualification. Thus several of the 'civilised' characters in the play, who have benefited from 'nurture' are shown to be variously corrupt – Alonso, Antonio and Sebastian – or misguided – Gonzalo's egalitarian 'commonwealth' rests on the illogical premise that it could only exist if he were king. Likewise, the character of Caliban, who proves himself immune to the redeeming effects of civilisation, goes beyond the simple stereotype of the evil savage; his eloquent poetry, his love of music, his dreams and his suffering in enslavement all implicitly question the assumption that nature is inherently bad. At the end of the play there is some small sign that he may have learned something from Prospero's experiment, just as Prospero is forced to 'acknowledge', perhaps, some responsibility for Caliban.

THE SUPERNATURAL

The Tempest was written at a time when belief in the supernatural was widespread, indeed, King James I had written a treatise on magic in 1603. The Jacobeans had identified two kinds of witchcraft, that which was practised by 'white witches', magicians whose powers were supposed to be derived from God, and 'black witches' who were disciples of the devil and used their powers for evil purposes. In *The Tempest*, Prospero is an example of the former and Caliban's mother, Sycorax, is an example of the latter.

The entire action of *The Tempest* is propelled by forces outside the laws of commonsense reality. Unlike *Macbeth*, where the witches influence the hero's fate but do not determine it, the outcome of *The Tempest* is entirely the product of Prospero's magic powers. The royal court may have been brought to the island 'by accident most strange' (I.1.178), but once within the reach of Prospero's power, their fate belongs to him. Because of this Shakespeare is able to concentrate attention on certain thematic interrelationships:

- The island is an isolated magical realm where King Alonso and his court have no authority, so authority becomes an issue
- Supernatural events force many of the characters to question the appearance of what they see, thus magic implements **metaphorically** (see Literary Terms) the process of self-knowledge and true recognition which takes place at the end

Prospero's magic is not all-powerful: it does not effect a change in the hearts of Antonio and Sebastian.

- Prospero's magic 'art' (I.2.25) symbolises the intellectual, moral and spiritual values of a superior form of civilisation
- Magic makes credible the immediate love between Ferdinand and Miranda.

FORGIVENESS OR REVENGE?

The rarer action is in virtue, than in vengeance (V.1.27–8)

The themes of love Will Prospero punish or forgive his enemies? This
and reconciliation question hangs in the air of the play until the final act.
are common to Yet by 'arranging' the marriage of his daughter to the
Shakespeare's final son of King Alonso, Prospero has surely prepared the
plays. way for reconciliation. The **masque** (see Literary
Terms) to celebrate the betrothal of the young people
emphasises the start of a new era and the hope of a new
generation.

MASTERS AND SERVANTS

There are several master/servant relationships in the
play, most of them unstable and characterised by some
form of resentment. Only Gonzalo demonstrates
consistent loyalty to his master, as he had done to
Prospero before the play starts:
- The boatswain challenges the authority of the king
  and his court
- Ariel is an unwilling servant and longs for freedom,
  which Prospero promises if he is obedient
- Caliban's first appearance in the play expresses a deep
  resentment for Prospero, who has enslaved him
- Antonio and Sebastian, though technically not
  servants, challenge the rightful authority of kings by
  planning to murder Alonso
- Stephano, butler to King Alonso, assumes the role of
  king and takes Caliban as his servant who urges him
  to kill Prospero
- Ferdinand is compelled to perform menial labour for
  Prospero.

All of these echo the issues of usurpation and rightful
authority which run through the play and which form
the motive for Prospero's action.

The fundamental shape of the plot heads towards the reversal of Prospero's fortunes; this 'shaping' of the story is integrated into the action.

The Tempest follows the conventional five-act structure of the Elizabethan and Jacobean drama. Within this framework there are ten scenes, which allow Shakespeare to develop different strands of the action and alternate the audience's attention from one group of characters to another and to simulate the passage of time. The play contains the following plots (see Literary Terms):

- The relationship between Ferdinand and Miranda
- The experiences of the royal court: the plot to kill Alonso
- Caliban, Stephano and Trinculo: the plot to kill Prospero.

All three strands of the play are controlled by the activities of Prospero and his servant, Ariel. In Act I we are given the immediate cause of the action, the shipwreck. This is followed by an exposition of past events – Prospero's conversation with Miranda – which provides the audience with important information about how they came to be on the island. The histories of both Ariel and Caliban are also given. The plot featuring Ferdinand and Miranda is begun.

Act II develops the theme of usurpation and authority through the activities of Antonio and Sebastian and the comic **sub-plot** (see Literary Terms) featuring Caliban, Stephano and Trinculo.

Act III intensifies the three plots by:
- Ferdinand agreeing to marry Miranda
- Caliban persuading Stephano and Trinculo to kill Prospero
- The climatic appearance of Ariel to denounce Alonso et al of their crime against Prospero.

Act IV begins the movement towards a final resolution when Prospero agrees that Ferdinand and Miranda can marry and the wedding **masque** (see Literary Terms) is performed. The plot against Prospero by Caliban, Stephano and Trinculo is foiled by Ariel.

In Act V the end of the play is marked by:
- The revelation of Prospero and his act of forgiveness
- The appearance of Ferdinand and Miranda playing chess
- The restoration of Prospero's dukedom
- The freeing of Ariel
- Prospero's epilogue.

However, in *The Tempest* the main plot concerns the actions of Prospero to undo the wrong that has been done to him and his daughter. Consequently, the three narrative strands identified above are subordinate to, and dependent upon, his actions. This gives the play a certain structural simplicity and focus, an aspect which is reinforced by its close adherence to the **classical unities** (see Literary Terms) of time, place and action:

Time

Prospero intends that his 'project' shall be completed in the space of a single afternoon: 'The time 'twixt six and now [about noon] / Must by us both be spent most preciously' (I.2.240–1). In Act V there are two more references to time, lines 3–4 and line 186, which remind us of his original intention and the speed with which it has been accomplished.

Place

Apart from the shipwreck in the first scene, the action of the play takes place in a single location, the island.

Action

The third unity required that a drama should have only one main **plot** (see Literary Terms). This is accounted for by the way the entire play evolves from Prospero's intentions; all the incidents in it are subordinate to this impulse.

PROSPERO

Loyal father

*Poised to take
revenge on his
enemies*

*A demanding
master of two
servants*

*Authority figure
who achieves
understanding
and forgives his
enemies*

Prospero's name is an indication of his function in the play. It is Latin for 'I cause to make prosperous, happy and successful'. By the end of the play he has brought love to Miranda and Ferdinand, restored his dukedom, forgiven his enemies, freed Ariel and promised a safe journey home to Italy for King Alonso and his court. However, in the course of the action we learn several things about Prospero which might qualify a view of him as merely a benevolent old man. Our first sight of him is as a father and a magician. We see his love and care for his daughter, Miranda, and the spectacular magic power he commands. We find out about his love of learning and how the selfish pursuit of 'secret studies' caused him to neglect his responsibilities as Duke of Milan. He explains that this unworldliness made him mistake the character of his brother, Antonio, whom he had trusted greatly. At the start of the play he is a troubled figure, angry and resentful.

A harsh side to his character is revealed in his dealings with his two slaves, Ariel and Caliban. Both are kept in his service under threat of painful punishment and although he feels love for Ariel, Caliban is treated with severe contempt. Towards the latter, he is like an authoritarian teacher who has failed to educate a difficult pupil; he believes Caliban can only be controlled by violence, 'whom stripes may move, not kindness' (I.2.47).

Power, in fact, is the key to Prospero's character. He lost one kind of power, the political and social power, when Antonio took his dukedom from him. He uses the power he gained from study, the power of knowledge, his magician's 'art', to regain that lost human status. This experience gives him a kind of melancholy wisdom; he shows insight into the importance of love and forgiveness, and an awareness of mortality. At the end, he knows he must renounce the 'rough magic' of the sorcerer so that he can resume his human destiny, 'where / Every third thought shall be my grave' (V.1.310–11).

CALIBAN

Second to Prospero, Caliban is probably the most important character in the play. He is certainly one of the most interesting characters Shakespeare ever created. This is partly because it is not clear how the dramatist saw him. He is part man and part beast, a mixture of tragic humanity and bestial wickedness. In the history of stage performances he has been played to resemble several kinds of animal, even a tortoise, and in earlier centuries was often played simply for laughs.

'A salvage and deformed slave'

At first he loved Prospero

Cunning

Naive

Capable of self-knowledge

In the **Folio edition** (see Literary Terms) he is described as 'a salvage and deformed slave'. In Shakespeare's times 'salvage' did not carry the same primary meaning as its modern form 'savage'. It meant 'wild and uncivilised', so in the Elizabethan hierarchy which moved from God down to inanimate nature, the uncivilised man was an inferior being. To Shakespeare's original audience Caliban's deformity would also signify wickedness, a belief emphasised by Prospero when he says that the slave's birth was the result of an association between his mother, the witch Sycorax, and the devil, (I.2.321–2). Caliban's name could be an anagram of 'Canibal' or a derivation from 'Cariban', the name given to Carib Indians. Either way, Caliban seems to embody an 'otherness' which serves as a contrast to the 'civilised' Europeans who come to the island.

In Act I Caliban refers to his friendship with Prospero when the magician first came to the island with his

Caliban is the
child of a devil
and a witch
(I.2.321–2).

daughter. Their relationship was reciprocal at that time, Prospero teaching Caliban his language, and Caliban in return showing Prospero 'all the qualities o' th' isle' (I.2.339). This harmonious relationship was broken when Caliban tried to rape Miranda. When we first see him he is a bitter, enslaved figure who regrets that he had not been able to father many Calibans from Miranda. He regards Prospero as a usurper who has taken the island from him.

Caliban has endured years of physical torture by Prospero, yet though his body has submitted to slavery, his mind is active and rebellious. He was intelligent enough to learn Prospero's language and he knows the consequences if he disobeys him: 'I must obey: his Art is of such pow'r, / It would control my dam's god, Setebos' (I.2.374–5). In his dealings with Stephano and Trinculo, he shows that he clearly understands the source of Prospero's power: 'First to possess his books; for without them / He's but a sot' (III.2.90–1). And, unlike his companions, he is not taken in by the flashy clothes hung up to distract them: '… it is but trash' (IV.1.224).

Caliban's unfamiliarity with Europeans other than Prospero and Miranda causes him to be easily impressed by Stephano and his 'celestial liquor'. He has been conditioned to serve by Prospero and the more he drinks Stephano's wine the more craven he becomes: '… I will kiss thy foot' (II.2.149). To King Alonso's servants Caliban is merely a 'monster', an exploitable savage; to Caliban, these strangers might have 'dropp'd from heaven' (II.2.137), and he foolishly believes they can free him from his servitude.

Caliban's natural intelligence makes him quick to see how he has misjudged Stephano and Trinculo: 'What a thrice-double ass / Was I' (V.1.295–6). Unlike Antonio and Sebastian, who express no remorse for their wickedness, Caliban at least recognises that he needs to be pardoned, even though this must be sought within the context of service to Prospero. In the moral scheme of the play he has proved himself to be less evil than Antonio and Sebastian, who plotted to kill Alonso to achieve power. Caliban's motive for planning to kill Prospero was to gain the freedom to live on the island which he has always believed belongs to him.

ARIEL

An obedient servant

'Moody'?

Instructs Prospero in human kindness

Provider of music

Ariel is not a person but a spirit, therefore his character is relatively simple. As his name implies, his element is air. At Prospero's bidding he moves through the play in a variety of disguises, sometimes invisible to the other characters.

Unlike Caliban, Ariel is keen to do Prospero good service because if he does he knows he will be freed at the end of it. This gives his attitude to Prospero a certain child-like quality, eager to please and anxious to remind his master of his loyalty and skill. For this Prospero treats him with affection.

Ariel has good reason to be grateful to Prospero. At the start of the play we learn how he was imprisoned by Sycorax for refusing to obey her commands, and how Prospero released him. Prospero is a better master, but he is still a master, and Ariel longs for freedom. To bring him to heel, Prospero has to remind him of the debt he owes his master and the 'art' which freed him from his painful imprisonment. Ariel promises to do all that Prospero commands 'gently', that is, carefully and correctly, otherwise Prospero will torture him with imprisonment for twelve years.

Although he is non-human, Ariel points Prospero towards a compassionate view of his enemies when he describes their suffering at the start of Act V. If Ariel symbolises Prospero's imagination, as some commentators believe, then it is at this point, lines 20–8, that Prospero makes the imaginative leap to sympathise with others of his 'kind' and show the 'virtue' of forgiveness.

Ariel contributes four songs to a play in which music is an important and integral part of the action. All four songs are relevant to the immediate events:

- I.2.377–83 – this song leads Ferdinand towards Miranda
- I.2.399–405 – a song which persuades Ferdinand that his father, Alonso, is dead
- II.1.295–300 – Ariel's song wakes up Gonzalo and alludes to the 'open-ey'd conspiracy' of Antonio and Sebastian
- V.1.87–94 – Ariel's promised freedom approaches and he sings in joyful anticipation as he dresses Prospero in the hat and cloak of the Duke of Milan.

MIRANDA

One who is admired

Compassionate and beautiful

Simple and direct

Miranda is about fifteen and has spent twelve years on the island in the company of her father, Prospero. She is adored by her father, who describes her as a 'cherubin' who gave him the courage to endure the hardships they experienced before arriving on the island. Since then, Prospero has devoted himself to her education.

The fruits of this careful nurturing are evident from Miranda's first speech in the play. She is able to show sympathy for the people in the shipwreck – 'O, I have suffered / With those that I saw suffer!' (I.2.5–6) – and she is kind to Ferdinand when he is carrying Prospero's logs. This inner goodness is reflected by her outer beauty. Both Ferdinand and Alonso believe she is a

'goddess' (I.2.424) when they first encounter her, and
Caliban describes her as a 'nonpareil' (III.2.98) of
beauty.

Miranda has only known two men in her life, Prospero
and Caliban, and this contributes to her rather
innocent forthrightness when she meets and falls in
love with Ferdinand. She offers to be his wife in
Act III after having known him for only a short time.
Her decision to speak of her desires in the language
of 'plain and holy innocence' (III.1.83) is an indication
of her moral stature in the play. All her encounters
are characterised by this simple honesty, even on
the only occasion when she speaks harshly (of
Caliban): ''Tis a villain, sir, I do not love to look on'
(I.2.311–12).

Because she is the only female in the play, Miranda
illuminates the themes of love and reconciliation. In
this sense her role is somewhat functional; her purpose
is to symbolise the positive effects of 'nurture' as
it contrasts with 'nature' in Caliban. It is worth
noting that Prospero refers to her as his 'gift' and
Ferdinand's 'acquisition worthily purchas'd' (IV.1.13) –
metaphors (see Literary Terms) that allude to the
political and economic motives behind arranged
marriages.

FERDINAND

Good looking and
brave
Fortitude
A loyal son

Miranda is so impressed by Ferdinand's good looks
when she first sees him that she thinks he is 'A thing
divine' (I.2.421). His outer beauty is an indicator
of his moral worth and a vivid image of him is provided
by Francisco when he describes how bravely Ferdinand
struggled with the sea after his shipwreck: 'his bold
head / 'Bove the contentious waves he kept'
(II.1.113–4).

Ferdinand gains Prospero's approval by the way he behaves during his imprisonment. His love for Miranda is deep and powerful so the menial tasks he is required to perform become dignified by thoughts of her.

Because he believes his father has perished in the wreck, Ferdinand assumes he must now be King of Naples (I.2.436–7). But this gives him no pleasure; his grief at his father's apparent death is genuine, as is the joy he expresses when, in Act V, he discovers that Alonso is alive.

Ferdinand is the perfect match for Miranda. His courage, nobility and kindness emphasise Prospero's intention to show love triumphing in a union of 'two most rare affections'.

ALONSO

A weak sinner capable of remorse

A grieving father

An active conscience

King Alonso has been an old enemy of Prospero who helped Antonio usurp him from the dukedom of Milan. He allowed himself to be manipulated by Antonio and cruelly permitted Prospero and his young daughter to be cast adrift at sea where they were expected to die, their fate kept secret from the people of Milan, who loved Prospero and would have revolted against Antonio if he had openly killed his brother to gain the dukedom.

Alonso has therefore sinned against Prospero, but his sin is not as strong as Antonio's because the crime against Prospero originated in the mind of Antonio. Shakespeare implies certain positive qualities in Alonso which make credible the restoration of rightful authority at the end of the play and the union between Miranda and Ferdinand, Alonso's son.

In spite of the considerable fatigue and despair he must feel, Alonso persists in trying to find Ferdinand, whom he grieves for openly and describes to the blaming Sebastian as 'the dear'st o' th' loss' (II.1.132).

After Alonso is confronted with his crimes by Ariel he expresses his deep sense of guilt and remorse in language which vividly evokes his disturbed conscience and self-hatred (III.3.95–102). At the end of the play he quickly restores Prospero's dukedom to him, showing true humility in asking both Prospero and Miranda to forgive him. His function in the play is therefore to demonstrate the necessity of true repentance based on a full knowledge of sin. King Alonso has been morally and spiritually cleansed by his experiences, and this makes way for the new beginning symbolised by the betrothal of his son to Prospero's daughter.

GONZALO

Optimistic
Loyal and just
Innocence of heart

Gonzalo is mocked by Antonio for being too talkative and this 'noble Neopolitan' (I.2.161), as Prospero calls him, provides comment on a number of incidents in the play.

In spite of the disastrous event that has occurred, Gonzalo insists that they will not drown because the boatswain had the appearance of a man who was born to be hanged, not drowned (I.1.28–30). Gonzalo means well, but his determination to look on the bright side does not go well with Alonso, who eventually pleads with him to be quiet (II.1.9).

It is Gonzalo's strong sense of justice that made him provide Prospero and Miranda with the necessities for survival when they were cast adrift in a leaking boat. This was done even though he owed no particular allegiance to Prospero. Gonzalo's sense of what is fair is further reflected in the way he criticises Sebastian for his insensitive treatment of Alonso. His loyalty to the king is absolute and when Ariel wakes him up to warn him of danger his immediate thought is for the king's safety: 'Now, good angels, Preserve the King!' (II.1.302–3)

Only the 'three men of sin' (III.3.53), Alonso, Antonio and Sebastian, hear Ariel's denunciation in Act III Scene 3. Gonzalo's response to the 'strange shapes' bringing in the banquet is full of simple wonder, even admiration, and he makes a telling comment when he observes that the manners of these creatures 'are more gentle, kind' (III.3.32) than those of humans. It is appropriate that this noble, honest and humane counsellor should be the one who pronounces the happy resolution of the story (V.1.205–13).

ANTONIO

Ruthless absence of conscience

Calculating and fearless

Prospero loved his brother, Antonio, almost as much as he loved Miranda. Antonio was entrusted to carry out Prospero's affairs of state and eventually started to behave as if 'He was indeed the duke' (I.2.102–3). When he schemed to have Prospero banished, Antonio was quite prepared to kill his brother and Miranda. Antonio's betrayal of Prospero is thus the root cause of the play's action.

Antonio is quite frank about his lack of conscience when Sebastian brings up the subject of Prospero (II.1.265–75). A true Machiavellian, he lures Sebastian to kill his brother by a process of shrewd psychological insight and ruthless practicality: knowing that Gonzalo would not support them he urges Sebastian to kill him too.

Antonio is a nobleman, educated and witty, but he is ruled by a lust for power and cannot empathise with other human beings. At the end of the play, even though he has been forgiven by Prospero, he has no

part in the general happiness. He remains unrepentant
and mostly silent.

SEBASTIAN

Courageous and
cynical
Incapable of
human sympathy

Sebastian is Alonso's brother and the friend of Antonio.
It is clear that he had some part in the usurption of
Prospero from Ariel's words 'you three / From Milan
did supplant good Prospero' (III.3.69–70).

Although Sebastian is similar in character to Antonio –
both engage in the cynical mockery of Gonzalo – his
wickedness is more passive than his friend's. It is
Antonio who arouses his ambition and persuades him
to abandon all thoughts of conscience; this Sebastian is
more than willing to do.

Like Antonio, Sebastian shows signs of physical
courage: he is prepared to fight the spirits in Act III
Scene 3, 'But one fiend at a time' (line 102). But, also
like Antonio, he expresses no remorse for his
wickedness in the final scene, even though he too is
forgiven by Prospero. Both characters are 'civilised' and
educated noblemen whose actions implicitly question
any assumption that Caliban's is the only type of
wickedness.

STEPHANO

Exploitative and
mercenary

Stephano is Alonso's butler. After the shipwreck he
floated ashore on a barrel of wine. He is very fond of
wine and he is always drunk. With Trinculo, his
function in the play is to provide comic relief.

When he first sets eye on Caliban, Stephano is quick to
think of the money he could make by taking this
'monster' home with him and selling him as a freak.
Stephano proceeds to get Caliban and Trinculo as
drunk as himself, and soon takes on the role of leader.

He believes his master, King Alonso, and all the court, have drowned. When Caliban tells him about Prospero, he decides to kill him and become king of the island, with the beautiful Miranda as his queen. Stephano is a greedy fool and a drunkard, as Caliban realises at the end of the play.

TRINCULO

Trinculo also thinks Caliban could be a profitable investment, especially if he took him to England as an exhibit: 'any strange beast there makes a man' (II.2.31–2). He does not like Caliban at all and is obviously afraid of him. Trinculo is Alonso's jester, so his comments have a mocking, critical edge which make him seem rather detached even when he is drunk.

Trinculo is just as greedy as Stephano and he is equally taken in and distracted by the flashy clothes in Act IV Scene 1. Also, like Stephano, he shows few signs of remorse at the end of the play.

LANGUAGE & STYLE

The Tempest is one of Shakespeare's last plays and its language reflects his mature understanding of poetic verse drama. Although the play does not contain the wealth of **imagery** (see Literary Terms) to be found in earlier works, there is an emphasis on certain important thematic ideas which are relevant to the situations depicted in the **plot** (see Literary Terms). It is a relatively short play with a sense throughout that Shakespeare is making every word and line count.

Blank verse   **Blank verse** (see Literary Terms) is used in the play for its normal purposes, that is, to heighten the importance of the ideas and emotions, and to reflect the higher

status of certain groups of characters. However, one
character of low status, Caliban, speaks in blank verse
almost all the time.

Prose

Prose (see Literary Terms) is spoken by the characters
either when important information is given to help the
audience's understanding of the plot, such as Gonzalo's
comments Act II Scene 1 lines 66–8, or when it is
spoken by low-status characters, usually within the
context of a comic **sub-plot** (see Literary Terms), such
as the speeches of Trinculo and Stephano.

Diction

The Tempest is notable for its use of key words
connected with the themes of the play. Thus we find
recurring references to 'nature' – 'barren ground – long
heath, brown furze' (I.1.65), 'fresh-brook mussels,
withered roots, and husks' (I.2.465), etc. Or there are
the group of words which evoke the importance of the
sea in the play – 'Sea-sorrow' (I.2.170), 'sea-change'
(I.2.403), 'still-closing waters' (III.3.64), and so on.
There are also many examples of words repeated to
emphasise the themes of 'beauty', 'nobility', 'virtue', and
there are images drawn from the theatre and acting in
the speeches of Antonio and Prospero. Another feature
of Shakespearean **diction** is the extensive use of **puns** or
word play (see Literary Terms). This usually occurs in
the comic scenes since the literary technique of playing
with the different meanings of words gave Elizabethan
and Jacobean audiences much intellectual amusement.
There are also examples of word play with a more
serious purpose, such as when Prospero uses two
meanings of 'key' when describing Antonio's
deviousness (I.2.83–5).

Soliloquy

Both Caliban and Ferdinand have **soliloquies** (see
Literary Terms) in which they reveal to the audience
what is going on in their minds while alone on the
stage (II.2.1–14 and III.1.1–15). However, unlike many
of Shakespeare's major characters, Prospero does not

usually employ this form of dramatic convention for this purpose.

Sometimes Prospero is made to employ a soliloquy to indicate another stage in his 'project', e.g. Act III Scene 1 lines 92–6, or to comment on the action while he is on stage but invisible to the other characters, e.g. Act V Scene 1 lines 33–57. Yet nowhere does Prospero reveal to the audience his inner motivation. It is not until the last act that we learn that he is going to forgive his enemies.

Dramatic
irony

The audience is made aware of the significance of an action or a piece of language when the characters do not share this awareness. Thematically, *The Tempest* is governed by the irony contained in a comparison between the behaviour of such characters as Antonio and Sebastian and their appearance as noblemen. This is given its most pointed form when Miranda exclaims 'O brave new world, / That has such people in't' (V.1.183–4).

PART FOUR

Study skills

How to use quotations

One of the secrets of success in writing essays is the way you use quotations. There are five basic principles:

- Put inverted commas at the beginning and end of the quotation
- Write the quotation exactly as it appears in the original
- Do not use a quotation that repeats what you have just written
- Use the quotation so that it fits into your sentence
- Keep the quotation as short as possible

Quotations should be used to develop the line of thought in your essays.

Your comment should not duplicate what is in your quotation. For example:

> Miranda says that she has suffered for the ship's passengers: 'O, I have suffered/With those that I saw suffer!'.

Far more effective is to write:

> Miranda's capacity for human sympathy is evident from the start: 'O', I have suffered/With those that I saw suffer'.

Always lay out the lines as they appear in the text. For example:

> Caliban feels deep resentment towards Prospero's attempt to educate him, 'The red plague rid you / For learning me your language!'.

However, the most sophisticated way of using the writer's words is to embed them into your sentence:

> When Miranda sees the 'goodly creatures' of this 'brave new world' she does not realise that some of them are wicked.

When you use quotations in this way, you are demonstrating the ability to use text as evidence to support your ideas.

Everyone writes differently. Work through the suggestions given here and adapt the advice to suit your own style and interests. This will improve your essay-writing skills and allow your personal voice to emerge.

The following points indicate in ascending order the skills of essay writing:
• Picking out one or two facts about the story and adding the odd detail
• Writing about the text by retelling the story
• Retelling the story and adding a quotation here and there
• Organising an answer which explains what is happening in the text and giving quotations to support what you write

....

• Writing in such a way as to show that you have thought about the intentions of the writer of the text and that you understand the techniques used
• Writing at some length, giving your viewpoint on the text and commenting by picking out details to support your views
• Looking at the text as a work of art, demonstrating clear critical judgement and explaining to the reader of your essay how the enjoyment of the text is assisted by literary devices, linguistic effects and psychological insights; showing how the text relates to the time when it was written

The dotted line above represents the division between lower and higher level grades. Higher-level performance begins when you start to consider your response as a reader of the text. The highest level is reached when you offer an enthusiastic personal response and show how this piece of literature is a product of its time.

Coursework essay

Set aside an hour or so at the start of your work to plan what you have to do.

- List all the points you feel are needed to cover the task. Collect page references of information and quotations that will support what you have to say. A helpful tool is the highlighter pen: this saves painstaking copying and enables you to target precisely what you want to use.
- Focus on what you consider to be the main points of the essay. Try to sum up your argument in a single sentence, which could be the closing sentence of your essay. Depending on the essay title, it could be a statement about a character: Caliban is probably less wicked than Antonio and Sebastian. They are motivated to murder Alonso to achieve power, whereas Caliban plots to kill Prospero because he believes this will gain him his freedom; an opinion about setting: Miranda is the perfect product of Prospero's 'nurture'. She has been schooled in goodness and nobility of feeling; or a judgement on a theme: I believe the main themes of the play are forgiveness and reconciliation. Prospero uses his magic powers to arrange everything for this end, which is ultimately symbolised by the marriage of Ferdinand and Miranda.
- Make a short essay plan. Use the first paragraph to introduce the argument you wish to make. In the following paragraphs develop this argument with details, examples and other possible points of view. Sum up your argument in the last paragraph. Check you have answered the question.
- Write the essay, remembering all the time the central point you are making.
- On completion, go back over what you have written to eliminate careless errors and improve expression. Read it aloud to yourself, or, if you are feeling more confident, to a relative or friend.

If you can, try to type your essay, using a word processor. This will allow you to correct and improve your writing without spoiling its appearance.

Examination
essay

The essay written in an examination often carries more marks than the coursework essay even though it is written under considerable time pressure.

In the revision period build up notes on various aspects of the text you are using. Fortunately, in acquiring this set of York Notes on *The Tempest*, you have made a prudent beginning! York Notes are set out to give you vital information and help you to construct your personal overview of the text.

Make notes with appropriate quotations about the key issues of the set text. Go into the examination knowing your text and having a clear set of opinions about it.

In most English Literature examinations you can take in copies of your set books. This in an enormous advantage although it may lull you into a false sense of security. Beware! There is simply not enough time in an examination to read the book from scratch.

In the
examination

- Read the question paper carefully and remind yourself what you have to do.
- Look at the questions on your set texts to select the one that most interests you and mentally work out the points you wish to stress.
- Remind yourself of the time available and how you are going to use it.
- Briefly map out a short plan in note form that will keep your writing on track and illustrate the key argument you want to make.
- Then set about writing it.
- When you have finished, check through to eliminate errors.

To summarise,
these are the
keys to success:

- Know the text
- Have a clear understanding of and opinions on the storyline, characters, setting, themes and writer's concerns
- Select the right material
- Plan and write a clear response, continually bearing the question in mind

SAMPLE ESSAY PLAN

A typical essay question on *The Tempest* is followed by a sample essay plan in note form. This does not present the only answer to the question, merely one answer. Do not be afraid to include your own ideas and leave out some of the ones in this sample! Remember that quotations are essential to prove and illustrate the points you make.

Do you think it is possible to feel any sympathy for Caliban?

Introduction   This should clearly outline how you are going to deal with the question. It should briefly summarise Caliban's role in the play, the good and the bad qualities in his character, and your particular bias.

Part 1   Describe the aspects of Caliban's character and situation which could arouse sympathy:
- His enslavement to Prospero and the loss of his inheritance – the island on which he was born and clearly loves
- The contempt and loathing felt for him by Prospero, Miranda, Trinculo and Stephano
- His unspecified physical deformity and the way he is labelled a 'monster'
- His sensitive response to music and nature, his longing and his dreams of beauty expressed in poetic verse

- His intelligence, reflected in the way he recognises Prospero's books as the source of his power and his ability to see the worthlessness of the 'glistening apparel'
- His final appeal for pardon and acknowledgement of error.

Part 2   Describe the aspects of Caliban's character and situation which are unsympathetic:
- He tried to rape Miranda when she was an innocent and trusting child
- He feels no remorse for this
- His servile attitude to Stephano
- His plot to have Prospero brutally killed
- The way he tempts Stephano with the 'prize' of Miranda if he kills her father for him.

Conclusion   This will draw all the material you have used in the main body the essay together, but should not just reiterate everything you have written. You should summarise the evidence for your own particular opinion and provide appropriate qualifications, such as the fact that modern perceptions of Caliban differ from those of Shakespeare's original audience.

FURTHER QUESTIONS

Make a plan as shown above and attempt these questions.
1 How important is the **masque** (see Literary Terms) in Act IV to the themes of the play?
2 Describe the relationship between Prospero and Ariel.
3 Describe the character of Antonio as it is shown throughout the play and explain why he has so little to say in Act V.
4 What for you are the main themes of *The Tempest*?

5 Describe the character of Gonzalo. How does he
   contribute to our understanding of the play?
6 How does the **sub-plot** featuring Caliban, Trinculo
   and Stephano reflect aspects of the main **plot**
   (see Literary Terms)?
7 Compare the characters of Miranda and Caliban.
8 Describe the mixture of **tragedy** and **comedy**
   (see Literary Terms) in the play.
9 Explain the title of the play.
10 Explain the difference between 'nature' and 'nurture'
   with reference to the characters and situations in the
   play.
11 Discuss the human and the non-human aspects of
   Ariel and Caliban.
12 Examine the way the **classical unities** (see Literary
   Terms) influence the structure of the play.
13 Show how the contemporary issues and concerns of
   Shakespeare's time are reflected in the play.
14 Why does Prospero renounce magic at the end of
   the play?

PART FIVE

CULTURAL CONNECTIONS

BROADER PERSPECTIVES

The Tempest Since its first performance at the court of King James I
in performance *The Tempest* has always been one of Shakespeare's most
popular plays. Yet up to about the middle of the
nineteenth century stage performances of *The Tempest*
had only a slight resemblance to the play Shakespeare
originally wrote.

In *The Enchanted Island* of 1667 the play was rewritten
to give Caliban and Miranda sisters, and a new
character, Hippolito, Duke of Nantua, was introduced.
There were elaborate stage effects in this version, with a
marked emphasis on **comedy** (see Literary Terms),
dancing and singing. The character of Sebastian and
the **masque** (see Literary Terms) were excluded.

The Enchanted Island was the prototype for over two
hundred years of performances, each version calling for
more and more spectacle until the original play had
been almost reduced to a pantomime. The critic,
William Hazlitt, described one performance in 1815 as
'vulgar and ridiculous'.

In modern times, performances of *The Tempest* have
been based on Shakespeare's text, giving precedence to
its complexity of themes and language. Not surprisingly
in a century in which the issues of race and political
power have been so important, the figures of Prospero
and Caliban have aroused particular interest. In his
1970 production of *The Tempest* the director, Jonathan
Miller, gave the play a distinctly colonial interpretation,
showing a primitive culture being destroyed by
European invasion. He described Caliban as 'the
demoralised, detribalised, dispossessed, suffering field-
hand'.

Films

Try comparing some of the following film versions of *The Tempest*:
- *Tempest* directed by Paul Mazursky, 1982. A free adaptation of the story in which a contemporary New Yorker moves to a Greek island with his daughter.
- *The Tempest* directed by Derek Jarman, 1979. This British film mixes absurdist comedy, jazz and a variety of characterisations from different styles and epochs.
- *Prospero's Books* directed by Peter Greenaway, 1991. A film which equates Prospero with Shakespeare.
- *Forbidden Planet* directed by Fred M. Wilcox, 1956. A sci-fi version in which the island is a forbidden planet.

Books

Two famous island stories are relevant to *The Tempest*:
- *Robinson Crusoe* by Daniel Defoe (Penguin, 1965)
- *Lord of the Flies* by William Golding (Faber, 1954)

Colonialism

Bury My Heart At Wounded Knee by Dee Brown (Picador, 1975) is an account of the fate of the American Indian during the nineteenth century.

Shakespeare studies

Shakespeare's Later Comedies edited by D.J. Palmer (Penguin, 1971) is an anthology of modern criticism.

Shakespeare Our Contemporary by Jan Kott (Methuen, 1965) is an original interpretation of Shakespeare's plays concentrating on their relevance to the modern age.

allegorical characters in a narrative or description that are symbolic of something else

blank verse unrhymed iambic pentameter a line of five iambs

classical unities in Greek drama, one complete action, or events which take place within a single day or night

comedy a drama which ends happily

diction the choice of words in a work of literature

dramatic irony this occurs when the development of the plot allows the audience to possess more information about what is happening than some of the characters themselves

Folio edition the first edition (1623) of all Shakespeare's plays

genre the term for a kind or type of literature, e.g. comedy or tragedy

hyperbole a figure of speech reliant on exaggeration

iambic pentameter a line of five iambic feet. The most common metrical pattern found in English verse

imagery a word picture using a metaphor or a simile

masque a courtly dramatic entertainment which flourished in Europe during the late sixteenth and early seventeenth centuries. Music, poetry and dancing were all expensively combined in a loose plot, usually allegorical or mythological

metaphor a comparison between two different things, e.g. 'I have used thee, / filth as thou art'

metre this is the pattern of stressed and unstressed syllables in a line of verse

parody an imitation of a specific work of literature (prose or verse) or style

devised so as to ridicule its characteristic features

personification where things or ideas are treated as if they were human beings, with human attributes and feelings

plot the plan of a literary work

prose any language that is not patterned by the regularity of some kind of metre

pun a play on words; two widely different meanings are drawn out of a single word, usually for comic purposes

Quarto edition one of the early unauthorised editions of Shakespeare's plays

riddle a deliberately puzzling way of referring to an object or an idea

simile a figure of speech in which one thing is said to be like another, always containing the word 'like' or 'as'

soliloquy a dramatic convention which allows a character in a play to speak directly to the audience – as if thinking aloud about motives, feelings and decisions

sub-plot a subsidiary action running parallel with the main plot of a play or novel

symbol something which represents something else by analogy or association

tragedy a tragedy traces the career and downfall of an individual

tragicomedy a mixture of tragedy and comedy

wit originally meaning 'sense', 'understanding' or 'intelligence', the word came to refer to the kind of poetic intelligence which combines or contrasts ideas and expressions in an unexpected and intellectually pleasing way

TEST ANSWERS

TEST YOURSELF (Act I)

A 1 Boatswain *(Scene 1)*
... 2 Miranda *(Scene 2)*
3 Prospero *(Scene 2)*
4 Prospero *(Scene 2)*
5 Ariel *(Scene 2)*
6 Caliban *(Scene 2)*
7 Boatswain *(Scene 1)*
8 Sycorax *(Scene 2)*
9 Ferdinand *(Scene 2)*

TEST YOURSELF (Act II)

A 1 Sebastian *(Scene 1)*
... 2 Gonzalo *(Scene 1)*
3 Antonio *(Scene 1)*
4 Francisco *(Scene 1)*
5 Caliban *(Scene 2)*
6 Trinculo *(Scene 2)*
7 Ferdinand *(Scene 1)*
8 Antonio *(Scene 1)*
9 Stephano *(Scene 2)*

TEST YOURSELF (Act III)

A 1 Ferdinand *(Scene 1)*
... 2 Prospero *(Scene 1)*
3 Trinculo *(Scene 2)*
4 Caliban *(Scene 2)*
5 Caliban *(Scene 2)*

6 Ariel *(Scene 3)*
7 Alonso *(Scene 3)*
8 Ferdinand *(Scene 1)*
9 Stephano *(Scene 2)*
10 Sebastian *(Scene 3)*

TEST YOURSELF (Act IV)

A 1 Prospero *(Scene 1)*
... 2 Iris *(Scene 1)*
3 Prospero *(Scene 1)*
4 Trinculo *(Scene 1)*
5 Trinculo *(Scene 1)*
6 Caliban *(Scene 1)*
7 Ferdinand *(Scene 1)*
8 Ariel *(Scene 1)*
9 Caliban *(Scene 1)*
10 Ariel *(Scene 1)*

TEST YOURSELF (Act V)

A 1 Prospero *(Scene 1)*
... 2 Prospero *(Scene 1)*
3 Alonso *(Scene 1)*
4 Miranda *(Scene 1)*
5 Alonso *(Scene 1)*
6 Prospero *(Scene 1)*
7 Ariel *(Scene 1)*
8 Gonzalo *(Scene 1)*
9 Stephano *(Scene 1)*
10 Ariel *(Scene 1)*

York Notes – the Ultimate Literature Guides

York Notes are recognised as the best literature study guides.
If you have enjoyed using this book and have found it useful, you
can now order others directly from us – simply follow the ordering
instructions below.

HOW TO ORDER

Decide which title(s) you require and then order in one of the following
ways:

Booksellers
All titles available from good bookstores.

By post
List the title(s) you require in the space provided overleaf,
select your method of payment, complete your name and
address details and return your completed order form and
payment to:

> *Addison Wesley Longman Ltd*
> *PO BOX 88*
> *Harlow*
> *Essex CM19 5SR*

By phone
Call our Customer Information Centre on 01279 623923 to
place your order, quoting mail number: HEYN1.

By fax
Complete the order form overleaf, ensuring you fill in your
name and address details and method of payment, and fax it
to us on 01279 414130.

By e-mail
E-mail your order to us on awlhe.orders@awl.co.uk listing
title(s) and quantity required and providing full name and
address details as requested overleaf. Please quote mail
number: HEYN1. Please do not send credit card details by
e-mail.

York Notes Order Form

Titles required:

Quantity	Title/ISBN	Price

Sub total _____

Please add £2.50 postage & packing _____

(*P & P is free for orders over £50*) _____

Total _____

Mail no: HEYN1

Your Name _____

Your Address _____

_____

Postcode _____   Telephone _____

Method of payment

☐ I enclose a cheque or a P/O for £_____ made payable to Addison Wesley Longman Ltd

☐ Please charge my Visa/Access/AMEX/Diners Club card
Number _____ Expiry Date _____
Signature _____ Date _____

(please ensure that the address given above is the same as for your credit card)

Prices and other details are correct at time of going to press but may change without notice. All orders are subject to status.

☐ *Please tick this box if you would like a complete listing of Longman Study Guides (suitable for GCSE and A-level students)*

York Press

Longman

Addison Wesley Longman